THE
Jungle
Garden

THE Jungle Garden

PHILIP OOSTENBRINK

Photographs by Sarah Cuttle

filbert press

First published in 2021 by Filbert Press
filbertpress.com

Text © 2021 Philip Oostenbrink
Photographs by Sarah Cuttle except for those credited on page 219
Design by Studio Noel

A catalogue record for this book is available from the British Library
ISBN: 978-1-9997345-6-5

10 9 8 7 6 5 4 3 2   22 23 24 25 26 27 28 29

Printed in China

CONTENTS

Foreword

Since my inspirational gardening Granny gave me a packet of carrot seeds and trowel at the age of three, I have had a passion for the wondrous world of plants. With my teenage years approaching, combining with my red blood cells developing a distinct shade of green, I had the privilege of observing dramatic foliage plants in the wild. Till the day I pass on I shall never forget the hypnotically spiralling foliage of *Aloe polyphylla* bursting out of the seemingly inhospitable rocky outcrops in the mist-laden, rugged Drakensburg Mountains of Lesotho. My encounter with jungle foliage was intensified when I was kidnapped in 2000 whilst plant hunting for rare species of orchid. I was held for 9 months in the Darien Gap on the Panamanian/Colombian border, each day not knowing whether I would be executed. I am obviously not recommending the experience, but after being kidnapped my retinas were treated to the most biodiverse collection of foliage I have ever and will ever encounter as our well-armed murderous captors moved us to remote tropical locations untouched by the hand of mankind. This is Mother Nature's jungle garden.

In the ecstatic ecosystems of the cloud forest, my horticulturally blessed darting eyes were treated to the finger foliage of the banana passionflower suspended on 20-foot stems, humongous banana and heliconia leaves and the teasingly dissected greenery of cassava. Wowsers, the complex shades of green and the deliciously varied leaf formations totally blew me away. During my death-defying captivity (on 16 June 2000 I was given 5 hours to live), I distracted myself from a horrible tortuous murder by sketching in my diary a miniature botanical map of the world. My World Garden was born. Today, as well as flowers to fill my miniature botanical world, heaps of species endowed with diversely dramatic foliage dominate the garden.

Having an uncontrollable passion for plants is a delightful leveller and Philip epitomizes the enthusiast plantsman: willing to share his knowledge, generous with his plants (my collection of *Aspidistra* is rapidly expanding!) but above all someone who makes you feel that you are not alone in your quest for pushing botanical boundaries. Plants create great friendships and although I have only known Philip for a few years, it feels like I have known him since childhood.

The Jungle Garden is a masterclass in enthusing an audience of all levels of plant knowledge, whatever growing space you are blessed with and illustrates that the rules of gardening are there to be broken, whether pushing boundaries of hardiness, aspect, soil or particularly in this context plant combinations (deliberate or accidental!). Personally, page 63 got my chlorophyll pumping when Philip states that 'striking combinations can be made when using plants originating from areas with the same growing conditions' – this is crucial to cultivating exotic foliage plants. Observing plants in the wild to improve your husbandry is the botanical backbone of my lifelong ethos.

May I wish you Happy Jungle Gardening and thank you, Philip, for taking the current surge of interest in tropical foliage to greater heights.

Tom Hart Dyke

Curator of The World Garden at Lullingstone Castle

CHAPTER 1

Intro—
duction

Influences in life mean that as a gardener you are drawn to certain features or designs and will adapt these for use in your own garden. Although my taste in plants has changed over the years, there has always been one central key design feature: making combinations that focus on foliage rather than flowers. A jungle garden is the culmination of a garden designed with foliage in mind.

About me

Gardening is in my genes. My first childhood memories are of working in my grandmother's garden with my father. We had an allotment for a few years and our home garden had a lot of lawn at first, but gradually this was converted into borders with brick paths cutting through them. I was fascinated with plants then and I am still fascinated with them now, which has resulted in a large collection, including four National Plant Collections: *Hakonechloa macra, Ophiopogon japonicus, Aspidistra elatior* and *A. sichuanensis* and variegated *Convallaria*, which I have displayed at the Hampton Court Flower Show several times.

My first plant collection was of *Sempervivum* and other alpine succulents; I must have been seven or eight when I started collecting these. I had a small rock garden along the drive and my uncle often supplied plants as he grew hardy succulents as a hobby. Later, I started to collect air plants, cacti and carnivorous plants, finding their textures and colours very appealing. Every week I would cycle to our local nursery to see what new succulent treasures had been delivered, always looking for something I didn't yet have. A neighbour was head gardener at a private institution and he would often teach me about gardens and spark my interest even more; the *Fuchsia magellanica* 'Alba' he gave me is still in my mother's garden today.

LEFT—Gardening is in my genes and even at a very young age I spent a lot of time outdoors tending the garden.

ABOVE—*Sempervivum arachnoideum* was one of the plants I grew as part of my first ever plant collection at the age of seven.

OPPOSITE—*Phormium tenax* (foreground) is a plant I started using a lot when I moved to the UK as I loved the tropical jungle look of it.

During my formal horticultural education I did some garden designing but my main interest was in borders and the range of plants I could combine within a variety of spaces. The college had a large garden where my best friend and I would study for our plant identification tests, often taking special note of unusual shapes of foliage. This did have one disadvantage in that the college was in an area of the Netherlands where temperatures could drop significantly in winter and often the gardens, including plant labels, would be covered in deep snow. For this reason, and because we had to warm up inside with tea a lot, I still struggle with conifer names as they would always be tested in winter.

After teaching horticulture at a secondary school for eight years I moved to the UK to start my own gardening business. Apart from doing general maintenance I also redesigned borders for clients. The range of plants used in the UK seemed very exotic to me and soon I started including plants such as *Trachycarpus*, *Phormium* and *Pittosporum* in my designs. In 2015, after three and a half years as deputy head gardener in a 4-hectare (10-acre) public garden, I was offered the job of Head Gardener at Canterbury Cathedral, where the gardens are very diverse in their planting. Palm trees and banana plants are framed by ancient flint walls and over the course of five years we added a range of other tropical plants and new introductions within the 9.3-hectare (23-acre) Precincts; the walls create a perfect micro-climate for tropical plants, which means plants such as bananas (*Musa*) can get through winter without any frost protection.

In March 2020, English Heritage offered me the position of Head Gardener at Walmer Castle and Gardens in East Kent, but five days later the UK went in lockdown due to Covid-19. It was time to work in my own garden and small nursery, and this period also gave me the opportunity to think about incorporating a jungle theme in the garden I would be overseeing next.

The start of

The first jungle garden I ever visited was Tresco Abbey Garden on the Isles of Scilly, where I spent a short break in 1998. Stepping off the tiny boat and into the Tresco garden made me feel as if I had just travelled thousands of miles to some Caribbean island. The plants around me were lush, large and tropical and I knew hardly any of their names. One plant I shall always remember from that visit is *Farfugium japonicum* 'Aureomaculatum', which has large green leaves, covered in yellow spots. It took me years to find it again, but eventually I saw it for sale at the Hampton Court Flower Show and immediately bought it.

Foliage has been an important part of any border I have designed, but in 2015 a visit to Norwich proved life-changing for me. After first visiting the beautiful Bishop's House, where big-leaved jungle plants such as *Tetrapanax papyrifer* 'Steroidal Giant' and *Musa basjoo* dominated some of the borders, I walked to Will Giles's Exotic Garden. It was closed for a wedding but, determined to see it after travelling halfway up the country, I went back later that same day to find it open for visitors again. The garden was unlike anything I had seen before. The scale of it and the way the garden was laid out with jungle plants made me feel as if I had travelled somewhere far from the British Isles rather than being behind an office block in East Anglia. Plant combinations were carefully considered, with different leaf textures and colours forming the base of each border. It was this garden that fuelled my love for jungle plants and has influenced my garden designs ever since.

Within weeks of my visit, Will Giles sadly died and his garden was never opened to the public again. I very much doubt my passion for jungle gardening could have been sparked anywhere else but in that amazing garden in Norwich, so I am forever grateful to whatever it was that made me decide to wait for it to reopen that day.

my jungle obsession

Other gardens in the UK that have inspired me are Abbotsbury Subtropical Gardens and Kew Gardens, as well as several private gardens that sometimes open for charity. Outside the UK, Juniper Level Botanic Garden in North Carolina, Edward VII Park in Lisbon and Karlostachys Jungle Garden in Normandy have been sources of plant ideas. At the village of Meeden in the Netherlands I discovered a nursery called Tuingoed Foltz which has an amazing jungle garden behind it. But of course inspiration can also be found in local garden centres and specialist nurseries where dedicated owners will often share their knowledge and experiences.

LEFT—Big leaves in shades of green combined with wooden or stone garden features give Abbotsbury Subtropical Gardens a very natural jungle look.

BELOW—The ruins at Tresco Abbey Garden make the area feel as if ancient buildings have been swallowed up by the jungle.

OPPOSITE AND ABOVE—Walking through the Palm House at Kew Gardens made me see how big jungle leaves could be combined. Although these plants have the protection of a glasshouse they inspired me to create similar effects outside.

Designing
with foliage

Designing a garden with foliage in mind doesn't mean you won't have any flowers in your garden at all; foliage plants can also flower, but the aim of a design like this is to have a mix of leaves that keep the garden interesting, even when the plants are not in flower. 'Mix' is the key word here. If a garden is designed with the leaf shapes, textures and colours in mind, it is important to avoid placing plants with similar foliage next to each other. Consider a field of wheat, for example; as beautiful as it is, the eye isn't drawn to anything in particular and cannot focus on individual shapes. However, if this field of wheat contains a large thistle, for instance, the focus will soon fall on that. The aim of this book is to explain how you can combine different plants for visual interest, understanding what works and why. It will also show you inspirational gardens which may give you ideas for a corner in your own plot.

Apart from aesthetics, another reason for incorporating more foliage in your garden is that leafy plants are among the best supports for all forms of insect life, especially species such as beetles, some of which live on the ground. With the numbers of invertebrates dwindling around the globe, it is important to support them as much as we can. Patches of lawn or paving will not provide habitat for invertebrates, but even placing some plants in pots along the edges of patios will be beneficial to them. This in turn means predators such as birds who feed on insects will also benefit. The wider the variety of plants grown, the better it is for wildlife and the use of evergreens will mean invertebrates such as ladybirds, who will feed on aphids, will have shelter during the winter months too.

There are many reasons to start a jungle theme in your garden, on your patio or even on a balcony. The most important reason of course is that a fully grown jungle garden just looks amazing. I hope this book will inspire you to try out some jungle plants and grow your own jungle space, whether it's big or small.

BELOW—Even in a small border the jungle look can be achieved by combining large leaves in contrasting shapes.

OPPOSITE—A mix of different kinds of foliage keeps the garden interesting and ensures it doesn't become a monotone, green background.

CHAPTER 2

Jungle Leaves

A jungle is a very diverse ecosystem, with an extensive range of plants that encompasses all kinds of foliage shapes, colours and textures. In a jungle garden at home, this effect can be replicated by planting a mixture of different species. Positioning them in borders throughout the garden, or planting up the boundary with a mix of foliage at different height levels, is a quick way to give the sense of being in a jungle.

Shapes and textures

The wide variety of leaf shapes and textures is the evolutionary result of them adjusting to temperatures, light conditions, water availability and the presence of foragers. In tropical jungles, where temperatures as well as humidity are high, plants tend to have larger leaves. The difference in leaf size between plant species in these jungles and other parts of the world is a result of less fluctuation in daytime and night-time temperatures, the amount of light and the availability of water. Plants which naturally grow in shade will try to capture as much sunlight as they can, which often results in larger leaf surfaces.

The texture of the leaves can be smooth and glossy or rough, hairy, spiny, dull, pleated or warty – also a result of evolution, as texture can be a deterrent to animals which graze on leaves, or designed to soak up as much water as possible where rainfall is only occasional. Texture may also be a protective layer to stop harsh sunlight from scorching the leaves, evidenced by a silvery, velvety surface or one that is succulent and thick-skinned.

LEFT—Plants have adapted to survive in climates with particular light levels, temperatures and rainfall. The fact that each plant has leaves of a different shape and texture is the result of evolution.

OPPOSITE—Spikes developed on plants such as this *Solanum atropurpureum* as protection against foragers.

THE JUNGLE GARDEN

Texture is as important as leaf shape when designing a garden; without different textures plants would merge into each other and the effect would be less interesting. A variety of textures is another way of making your eye wander through a garden, picking up something different. Leaf texture is also important for the tactility of a garden. Lamb's ear (*Stachys byzantina*), for instance, has soft, velvety leaves which are challenging to pass without stroking them.

While large, coarse leaves provide a bold structure to the garden, lighter and finer leaves give it airiness and a feeling of space as the light filters through them. This filtered light is something the Japanese are very conscious of and they have even given it its own name: *komorebi*. There is not a literal translation for this, but it describes the interplay between sunlight and leaves that you see when the sun shines through the canopy. This effect can be achieved very well with bamboos, but also with Japanese maples and *Aralia*.

OPPOSITE—The glossy surface of the fan-shaped leaves of *Trachycarpus fortunei* stand out more because of the matt surface of the hosta leaves below.

TOP LEFT—The leaves of *Schefflera macrophylla* have a rough and wrinkly texture, making them a good combination with smooth, glossy leaves.

TOP RIGHT—*Stachys byzantina* 'Big Ears' (bottom) has velvety leaves.

Seasonal changes

Japanese gardens often have good examples of plant combinations where the foliage takes precedence over flowers. Plants such as *Ophiopogon*, *Hosta* and pine trees are often used with great care and consideration, and every plant has to be worthy of inclusion to form a perfectly balanced space. An example of how important foliage is in Japanese culture is the term *momijigari*, which means visiting parks and wild nature to see the beauty of the leaves during Koyo (red leaf) season. *Momiji* means autumn-coloured foliage, but it has also become the name for Japanese maple, which is seen as having the most beautiful autumn display of all trees. Trips to see autumn leaves are not limited to Japan either. I remember my grandmother in The Netherlands talking about 'herfsttintentochten' (autumn-colour trips) which involved day trips by minibus through the countryside and woodlands to see the autumn leaves. And in the Northeast of the United States, in areas such as Maine and New Hampshire, autumn 'leaf-peeping' is a highlight in the fall calendar.

When designing a jungle garden, it is good practice to consider plants that change with the seasons. A garden planted solely with evergreens which are more or less the same in every season can be quite boring, for at no point are you keen to see how the garden has progressed. The excitement of seeing a plant that has newly emerged from the ground, or young leaves that unfurled bright white changing to a buttery yellow in autumn, are reasons to explore the garden for fresh delights. Introducing plants with good autumn colour also gives a sense of the passing of time; when the change of seasons goes unnoticed, a garden becomes static. Especially in built-up urban locations, where there is often more concrete than greenery, awareness of the unfolding of the seasons can be of great benefit to mental health.

OPPOSITE—*Miscanthus sinensis* and Japanese maples create a stunning autumn display which provides an extra layer of interest in the garden.

LEFT—*Sanicula epipactis* 'Thor' flowering in early spring indicates a new season of growth is about to start.

ABOVE—*Fritillaria imperialis* 'Aureomarginata' emerging in spring.

Leaf shape
lists

The range of leaf shapes is quite extensive, but for the
purpose of this book it has been divided into ten shapes,
the names of which often describe the form.

A palmate leaf is so named because it resembles an open hand, with the individual lobes of the leaf all starting from a central point. Examples of plants with palmate leaves are maples and horse chestnuts. Plants with this type of leaf make good combinations with most other plants, as the leaf shape is so different from other types they tend to provide contrast, especially with small, lanceolate or round leaves. Sometimes little climbers can be found scrambling through the large leaves, which gives a lovely contrast without taking up much more space.

Best palmate leaves

- *Acer palmatum*
- *Begonia luxurians*
- *Brassaiopsis mitis*
- *Cussonia paniculata*
- *Fatsia japonica* 'Tsumugi-shibori'
- *Ficus johannis* subsp. *digitata*
- *Kalopanax septemlobus*
- *Manihot grahamii*
- *Tetrapanax papyrifer* 'Rex'
- *Trevesia palmata*

Palmate

Linear

A linear leaf is one that follows a straight line without any branching, such as are found on grasses and *Phormium*. Linear leaves can be used to change the direction of how the eye travels through the garden. Often linear plants have a horizontal or pendulous habit which forms good combinations with more upright plants with larger leaves, the slender shapes forming small exclamation marks among them.

Best linear leaves

- *Aspidistra sichuanensis*
- *Convallaria majalis* 'Albostriata'
- *Dasylirion serratifolium*
- *Hakonechloa macra*
- *Kniphofia caulescens*
- *Liriope muscari* 'Okina'
- *Ophiopogon japonicus* 'Spring Gold'
- *Pseudopanax ferox*
- *Puya chilensis*
- *Setaria palmifolia*

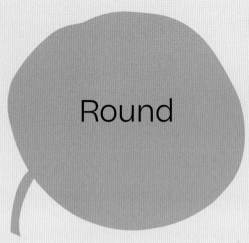

Round

A round leaf may have the leaf stalk in the centre, as in *Tropaeolum* (nasturtium), or further towards the edge of a leaf, for example *Farfugium*. Round leaves can look much like heart-shaped ones from a distance, so the two don't form a satisfying combination, especially when the colour and texture are very similar. Opposites of round leaves that make good combinations are plants with more pointed foliage such as those from the linear, palmate, filigree and fan-shaped groups.

Best round leaves

– *Astilboides tabularis*
– *Azara microphylla* 'Variegata'
– *Farfugium japonicum* 'Aureomaculatum'
– *Farfugium japonicum* 'Ryuto'
– *Tropaeolum majus*

Although the term 'filigree' does not exactly represent a leaf shape, it is the best way to describe the finely branched foliage of plants such as ferns and some conifers. These filigree leaves with their finer texture are good to use in planting schemes where a lot of larger leaves are present. They are ideal for weaving groups of large-leaved plants together and give coherence while at the same time providing the interruption that is needed to prevent everything blending in. The lace-like structure of a filigree leaf means other plants can easily grow through them and they won't suppress each other.

Best filigree leaves

– *Acer palmatum* 'Koto-ito-komachi'
– *Adiantum raddianum*
– *Athyrium filix-femina* 'Dre's Dagger'
– *Athyrium niponicum* var. *pictum* 'Ursula's Red'
– *Broussonetia papyrifera* 'Laciniata'
– *Dahlia* 'Woodbridge'
– *Dicksonia antarctica*
– *Eupatorium capillifolium*
– *Helianthus salicifolius*
– *Mahonia eurybracteata* subsp. *ganganpinensis* 'Soft Caress'

Filigree

Heart-shaped

A heart-shaped leaf is much like a round leaf except that there is a point at the end, which may be so small as to be barely visible at first. Lime trees (*Tilia*) can have perfect heart-shaped leaves, as can many cultivars of *Hosta*. Plants with heart-shaped leaves tend to be good in combination with plants from the filigree group. *Hosta* with ferns is a classic combination that has been used by the Japanese for centuries and it works very well because of the differences in texture as well as colour.

Best heart-shaped leaves

- *Begonia variegata*
- *Colocasia esculenta* 'Pink China'
- *Colocasia gaoligongensis*
- *Catalpa bignonioides* 'Aurea'
- *Catalpa x erubescens* 'Purpurea'
- *Hosta*
- *Sparrmannia africana*
- *Tolmiea menziesii* 'Taff's Gold'

The lance-shaped, or lanceolate, leaf tends to be quite elongated and pointy. It is somewhere between heart-shaped and linear forms but can form good combinations with either of them. Resembling a wide linear leaf, it can also be combined very well with palmate, fan-shaped, filigree and round leaves. The shape is quite close to that of paddle-shaped leaves, so if they are of similar size it is important to mix another plant with a different shape between them. *Persicaria* often has very defined lance-shaped leaves.

Best lance-shaped leaves

- *Castanea sativa* 'Variegata'
- *Cyrtomium fortunei*
- *Disporum longistylum* 'Night Heron'
- *Eriobotrya japonica* 'Okân'
- *Hedychium* 'Dr Moy'
- *Iresine herbstii*
- *Oreocnide pedunculata*
- *Persicaria microcephala* 'Red Dragon'
- *Tradescantia zebrina*
- *Zingiber mioga* 'White Feather'

Lance-shaped

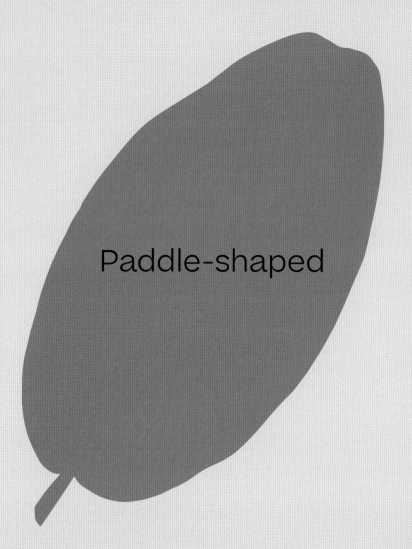

Paddle-shaped

Paddle-shaped foliage tends to be very elongated, with a central vein going the length of the leaf. Banana plants and *Strelitzia* have paddle-shaped leaves, though in the case of bananas the leaves often shred all along that central vein. This is to protect the plant from wind damage, so it is perfectly natural and offers a different texture in the garden when it occurs. Jungle plants with paddle-shaped leaves and an upright habit give height and structure to the garden. *Ensete* is a tender genus from the banana family and the upright, sometimes red, foliage stands out from the crowd. This is important for the variation in the garden as it will lead the eye vertically, instead of maintaining it horizontally at more or less the same level. Hardier *Canna* is another example of plants with paddle-shaped leaves. This genus comes in plants of all kinds of colours and sizes that will reach their height in one growing season.

Best paddle-shaped leaves

– *Canna 'Musifolia'*
– *Ensete ventricosum 'Maurelii'*
– *Musa basjoo*
– *Musella lasiocarpa*
– *Strelitzia reginae*

Fan-shaped

While a fan-shaped leaf is much like a palmate leaf, it lacks the individual lobes. This leaf form combines well with bold leaves, such as heart-shaped, paddle-shaped or round. The shape of some palmate leaves can be a bit too close to fan-shaped leaves, so when using these two near each other it is best to put a different plant in the mix, such as one with filigree leaves. The finer texture will then form a good enough contrast to make sure the difference in leaf structure stands out.

Best fan-shaped leaves

– *Adiantum venustum*
– *Chamaerops humilis*
– *Ginkgo biloba*
– *Hakea baxteri*
– *Sinopanax formosanus*

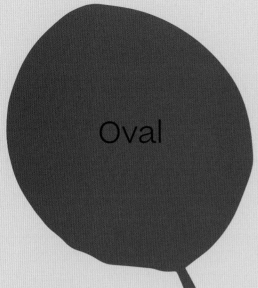

Oval

An oval leaf has the shape of an egg. Their curved form makes them less suitable to combine with rounded leaves but they form a great contrast with leaves that have pointed tips. These can be palmate, linear, feathered or the soft texture of filigree leaves. Plants with oval leaves can be found in genera such as *Cotinus* and *Rhododendron*.

Best oval leaves

- *Amicia zygomeris*
- *Cotinus coggygria*
- *Muehlenbeckia complexa* 'Tricolor'
- *Nicotiana glauca*
- *Plectranthus* 'Brunsendorf'
- *Reynoutria japonica* var. *compacta* 'Milk Boy'

This type of leaf has a central vein with leaflets on either side. At the tip of the leaf a single leaflet points lengthways. *Sorbus* and *Rhus* are popular plants with feathered leaves, but there are several other trees and shrubs which have this shape and some can be coppiced, making them suitable for smaller gardens and pots. Feathered leaves form a good contrast with palmate, round or heart-shaped leaves, their bold structure standing out against the individual feathered leaflets.

Best feathered leaves

- *Aralia bipinnata*
- *Coronilla valentina* subsp. *glauca* 'Variegata'
- *Dahlia imperialis*
- *Glycyrrhiza glabra*
- *Sorbus ulleungensis* 'Olympic Flame'
- *Melianthus major*
- *Rhus typhina* Tiger Eyes ('Bailtiger')
- *Robinia pseudoacacia* 'Lace Lady'
- *Sambucus nigra* f. *porphyrophylla* Black Tower ('Eiffel 1')
- *Tagetes lemonii*

Feathered

Variegation and variation

Variegation and variation are closely related and both are valuable in adding pops of colour to a planting scheme. A variegated leaf is one which has multiple colours while variation in a plant results in leaves of a uniform non-green colour (it might be yellow or purple for instance). These different colours can be caused by a genetically determined lack of a particular nutrient; even if the plant is given these nutrients in a fertilizer it is unable to absorb them. For this reason some people look upon variegated plants as being sickly, but even though the plant cannot benefit from the nutrients, it will still be able to flourish in your garden and add extra colour to borders and pot displays. Variegation can also be the effect of parts of a leaf being thinner than other parts. Quite often this is seen on foliage with a white edge where the green parts are thicker than the white, though sometimes these areas darken to green later in the year.

Variegation comes in different forms: it can be a margin around the leaf edge, stripes throughout the leaf, a marbled effect or even just random spots. The last is an example of evolutionary defence mechanisms. The markings are seen by foragers as existing damage and they will move on to other plants which do not look as if they have been eaten already.

OPPOSITE–Variegation on *Strobilanthes lactea*.

ABOVE–*Tradescantia zebrina* has variegated silver leaves with purple stripes. In shadier locations the leaves will be larger than when the plant is grown in a sunny position.

A jungle garden can greatly benefit from the use of variegated plants as they will add colour and texture to the planting scheme. It is yet another way of keeping your eye moving around the garden, following the colours, shapes and textures of leaves. However, overuse of variegation can have an adverse effect as the eye cannot rest on anything in particular and will bounce around the different colours so much that it cannot find a still space. By combining lighter leaves, such as yellows, with darker foliage the colours will enhance each other. The brighter foliage will stand out more as it contrasts with the dark, while the darker foliage will seem even darker and will give more depth to the border. Darker foliage near a variegated plant will also create a moment of calm and make the rest of the surrounding plants blend in better with the more vibrant plant.

ABOVE—The thin, yellow leaves of *Hakonechloa macra* 'All Gold' are valuable for their colour and shape and they move in the slightest breeze.

OPPOSITE—The central yellow variegation of *Fatsia japonica* 'Murakumo-nishiki' gives the leaves extra colour and interest.

THE JUNGLE GARDEN

Variegation can be bold and pronounced, but some variegated patterns can be very intricate and delicate. When the intricate pattern covers the entire leaf, the colour can seem uniform from a distance but as soon as the plant is seen up close the true markings are evident. This adds to the effect of surprise and interest which is so important in a garden. *Pelargonium* 'White Mesh' is a good example as its colour looks flat from further away, but on close examination the beautiful lace-like markings of the leaf become apparent and can be fully appreciated. Another fine example is *Strobilanthes dyeriana*, which from a distance seems a bright purple-leaved plant but up close the pattern as well as the beautiful

iridescence of the leaf can be seen. Plants such as these are not common garden plants and will excite the visitor, who will then want to explore other areas of the garden to see if there are more of these hidden treasures.

ABOVE—The intricate lace-like variegation of *Pelargonium* 'White Mesh' is more prominent when the plant is grown out of direct sunlight. From a distance it appears to be a very bright leaf, but when seen up close the full pattern become visible.

OPPOSITE—The purple colours on *Strobilanthes dyeriana* are unusual and iridescent when seen from different angles.

THE JUNGLE GARDEN

A common form of variegation is when the margin of the leaf has a different colour. This pattern is often caused by the leaf being thinner around the edges. Often these plants have 'marginata' in their botanical name. Leaves with this kind of variegation show off their leaf edge beautifully and will frame the green, or different coloured, centre. Plants with a different coloured margin will break up the leaf pattern in a garden and can stand out from the rest of the plants. It is good to use these as accent plants or, in the case of plants with white or yellow margins, in a darker corner where they will stand out and brighten up the area. Sometimes white on a leaf can scorch in too much sunlight, so this is another reason for these plants to be placed in areas of the garden with low light levels.

OPPOSITE—*Iresine herbstii* 'Acuminata' goes by the common name of bloodleaf which reflects the colour as well as the veins of the leaf.

LEFT—*Castanea sativa* 'Variegata' has a loose white margin which gives it a marbled effect. A plant like this can be placed in areas of the garden with low light levels, which will also ensure the white doesn't scorch and will retain its colour for longer.

ABOVE—*Begonia rex* 'Casey Corwin' has colour combinations of green, grey and pink. The brown edge accentuates the serration of the leaf. Begonias are easy to grow from a plug to a fully grown plant within one season.

Flowers in the jungle

Plants that are grown for foliage can of course also produce flowers. Some are insignificant, but on other plants they may be showy and bright. The colours and shapes of these flowers will provide extra interest throughout the year and will in turn invite people (as well as pollinators) to explore the garden further. Flowers come and go but it's the changing nature of gardens through the seasons that makes them exciting. Flowers may also provide scent in the garden and there are some plants that exude scent from their leaves too when you lightly brush past them on your walk through the garden. One such plant is *Tagetes lemmonii*, which is a shrubby French marigold. It produces small marigold flowers in winter and early spring and the scent of the feathered leaves is stronger than that of most flowers.

LEFT—The large, showy flowers of this *Brugmansia* x *flava* 'Mobisu' give off a sweet scent in the evening.

ABOVE—*Arisaema candidissimum* flowers from May onwards.

OPPOSITE—*Early flowering bulbs such as Iris* x *hollandica* 'Frans Hals' (Dutch iris) can work very well in a jungle garden. These plants will emerge and flower before the jungle foliage covers the ground and provide extra colour early in the year. By the time the jungle foliage has fully developed, the bulbs will have gone dormant and have stored enough energy to flower.

THE JUNGLE GARDEN

OPPOSITE—Flowering plants around this small clearing in the garden create a small colourful oasis.

LEFT—*Coronilla valentina* subsp. *glauca* 'Citrina' flowers almost all year. On sunny winter days the scent will drift through the garden.

BELOW—*Lobelia laxiflora* var. *angustifolia* produces red and yellow flowers with a tropical appearance.

Dots

and

smudges

Sometimes variegation does not take the shape of lines and edges but instead dots and smudges. These can be part of the plant's defence mechanism against foragers or just a random genetic occurrence which a plant breeder found attractive and grew on for gardens. Some plants are specifically bred to increase the number of dots on their foliage to add interest even when the plant is not in flower. Dots and smudges on leaves can greatly benefit the border design because their vivid patterning, often in bright colours, makes the display lively and interesting.

Plants with the word 'maculata' in their botanical name are often plants which have dots or speckles somewhere. 'Aureomaculatum' would mean the spots are of a golden colour, whereas 'Albomaculatum' means they are white. These spots are the result of a genetic mutation that means some parts of the leaves are unable to produce chlorophyll. Gardeners can use these plants with great effect as the pattern is often very different to other plants in the garden. Some plants are selected for having spots in their leaves to provide interest prior to flowering and *Zantedeschia* or calla lily is one such plant. They have attractive flowers in a wide range of colours, but often the leaves have beautiful patterns too, with white spots all over them. This makes the plant a talking point in the garden, long before the flowers are out. If we look at a plant with round leaves such as *Farfugium japonicum* 'Aureomaculatum', the bright yellow dots on its surface accentuate the shape of the leaf.

It gives greater emphasis to the round form which will be picked up almost subconsciously when viewing it. In areas with lower light levels, or in the evening, the yellow dots almost seem like small fireflies when a breeze stirs the leaf. This is another trigger for the senses which all adds to the garden being an interesting, changing entity.

BELOW—The bold, speckled leaves of *Zantedeschia aethiopica*.

BOTTOM—The dots on *Farfugium japonicum* 'Aureomaculatum' are bright yellow and almost look like a starry sky.

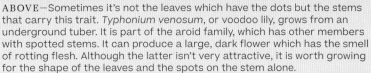

ABOVE—Sometimes it's not the leaves which have the dots but the stems that carry this trait. *Typhonium venosum*, or voodoo lily, grows from an underground tuber. It is part of the aroid family, which has other members with spotted stems. It can produce a large, dark flower which has the smell of rotting flesh. Although the latter isn't very attractive, it is worth growing for the shape of the leaves and the spots on the stem alone.

ABOVE RIGHT—The white pattern of this unusual *Ficus carica* 'Jolly Tiger' gives the leaf a marbled effect. Unlike other figs this plant can't be grown in full sunlight as the white will scorch and turn brown. In shade the colour will be retained and seem brighter.

RIGHT—*Podophyllum versipelle* 'Spotty Dotty' loves shade. The pattern on the leaf makes its shape even more prominent.

OPPOSITE—The white pattern on *Fatsia japonica* 'Tsumugi-shibori' resembles a spider's web.

The naturalistic jungle

One way of creating a jungle garden in its purest form is to use only green leaves; there are many shades of green among plants and when these different plants are combined, the colours will still stand out from each other. Variegated plants which are available in nurseries are often the result of selections made by plant breeders and don't exist in nature. There are many natural patterns and textures which provide a less artificial variation on the green theme and create a pleasing garden where slight nuances in texture and colour provide enough interest to make you feel as if you are immersed in a biodiverse jungle.

As variegated plants are often brought to market by a grower, they will usually have a cultivar name. One way to keep things natural and green is to avoid plants which have names such as 'Albomarginata', 'Variegata', 'Aureomarginata' and 'Argenteovariegata'. Plants without cultivar names are just plain species, which tend to be green forms. Of course, not all plants with cultivar names are variegated. *Tetrapanax papyrifer* 'Rex' is a cultivar with massive green leaves that enhances every jungle garden, even naturalistic ones, immensely.

A naturalistic jungle provides an opportunity to showcase the diversity of form and leaf shape which, in the case of just using green foliage, becomes even more important as it prevents the border from appearing as one green mass. Large, bold leaves need to be balanced by finer, more delicate foliage. Another way to create this natural balance is to provide a good upper canopy in the garden. Use large-leaved plants for this as they will create pockets of darkness allowing the lower levels and jungle floor to come alive, enhancing the natural feel of the garden.

OPPOSITE—In this purist's garden of green foliage plants, only species have been used.

ABOVE—The diversity in leaf shapes and textures, as well as the different shades of green, make this border very interesting even though there are neither flowers nor variegation.

THE JUNGLE GARDEN

OPPOSITE—This naturalistic jungle planting displays a pleasing balance of solid and feathery leaf structures. The spotted stem of the *Typhonium venusum* catches the attention.

ABOVE—The rigid, saw-toothed leaves of *Pseudopanax ferox* form a focal point in this border.

RIGHT—The underside of the leaf of *Ensete ventricosum* 'Maurelii' is a striking, very dark red. The upright, linear leaves of the *Eucomis comosa* hybrids in the foreground draw the eye up towards this main feature in the border.

Beyond the boundary

Most natural jungles seem endless, as dense vegetation continues far beyond what can be seen. Likewise, dense planting can make a garden seem much bigger, and using boundaries such as a fence to plant against can add to the effect. There are beautiful climbers such as *Akebia* or evergreen *Clematis* that will quickly form a vigorous structure along a fence or wall, or shrubs and bamboos can be planted along the edge to disguise the man-made boundary. The denser the vegetation, the more dark corners are created and dark-leaved plants in particular give the illusion of depth and space beyond what can be seen. Even a dark-green ivy on a fence, for instance, can make it seem as if more lies beyond.

Using a boundary structure which is of a darker colour can also enhance the sense of depth in a garden. Another great option is to create a living wall. Some older systems had only tiny compartments for the plants, which meant they would dry out quickly and require irrigation every day. Newer systems contain large pockets in which the plants can be placed, and some have shelves from which integrated pots are suspended, offering a vertical pot display.

BELOW—Dense planting behind the blue bench gives the impression that the planting carries on for miles but less than 1.5m (5ft) behind this bench is the neighbouring fence.

OPPOSITE—A garden fence covered in climbing plants such as x *Fatshedera lizei* is a good way to create a dense, green background to the garden which makes it seem as if there is more growth beyond the boundary. If the climbers are pruned and kept close to the fence they won't take up much space and are very suitable for even the smallest garden.

THE JUNGLE GARDEN

The minimalistic jungle

Not every area in a natural jungle is densely planted, and not every jungle garden has to be packed with plants to achieve a jungle effect. Some minimalist gardens still achieve the lushness of a jungle-themed garden just by placing large-leaved plants next to more delicate and airy plantings. After all, a garden is used for more than just a display of plants – areas to entertain or relax need to be included in the design. The jungle effect can be achieved by placing statement plants with large structures and bold leaf textures along the edges, and if they spread their crowns over any seating area this will add to the sense of being immersed in greenery. Light will be filtered by these tall boundary plants and what is beyond the boundary will be hidden by foliage, making it seem as if the garden is only the edge of the jungle and the denser vegetation lies beyond.

The patterning and shape of foliage in minimalist gardens is even more important than in densely planted gardens as it must be achieved with just a few plants. Bold opposites such as the *Tetrapanax papyrifer* 'Rex' and a large phormium work very well in a scenario like this for a relatively low cost. In the picture above the wonderful palmate leaf of the tetrapanax contrasts dramatically with the linear leaf of the phormium which in its variegated form brings an extra dimension.

OPPOSITE—In this small patio garden, large specimens of *Dicksonia antarctica* have been planted along the edges to create a jungle feel.

LEFT AND ABOVE—In a minimalistic garden, large statement plants such as *Musa basjoo* (left) or *Tetrapanax* and *Phormium* (above) will give an instant jungle effect.

Good combinations

＋

In order to achieve a diverse look in a jungle garden it is important to use a range of different leaf shapes. You don't need a big space to take a theme and develop it very well; no garden is ever too small to be interesting. If two plants with the same shape of leaf are near each other, try to place another plant with a different leaf shape between the them so that they don't just merge into each other.

As well as considering leaf shape, similarity in colour and texture of foliage requires attention too. To break up a consistent pattern, first think about introducing a different size of leaf; for example, if two plants have very large, round leaves, then a third with smaller, more linear foliage can weave the two together in a more interesting way. Don't be afraid to use large leaves in small gardens as, although the plant may take up more space, that type of layering ensures a jungle effect with almost instant impact. Even the smallest garden could have a *Tetrapanax papyrifer* 'Rex' if it is pruned every so often. This diverse look in a jungle garden is also a great way to entice people into the garden.

In this image below there are two shrubs with palmate leaves: *Fatsia japonica* and *Acer shirasawanum* 'Jordan'. The pairing offers a relatively nice combination because the size and texture are different. However, the small *Rhododendron* at the front makes for a far more pleasing image because the shape of that leaf is oval, contrasting with the pointy palmate leaves and almost at opposite ends of the spectrum in terms of leaf shape. Because the texture of both the *Fatsia* and *Rhododendron* leaves is similarly glossy, they pick up on each other and make the *Acer*, which has a matt yellow colour, stand out from them. An additional attraction to the *Rhododendron* is that this particular cultivar has foliage which emerges in a dark red colour in spring. The effectiveness of the combination of these three plants can be seen clearly when the round leaf of the *Rhododendron* is covered up and only the *Fatsia* and *Acer* are visible.

BELOW—*Fatsia japonica*, *Acer shirasawanum* 'Jordan' and *Rhododendron* 'Elizabeth Lockhart'.

THE JUNGLE GARDEN

Pictured left is a wall of ferns which was created in a narrow alleyway alongside the house, showing that even in a space of just over 1m (3¼) wide, it is still possible to create a jungle feeling. The ferns at the bottom are two *Polystichum* with a very similar leaf structure. The colour and size are marginally different and when the two mature, they will blend into each other. Above the two *Polystichum* is a crested *Asplenium* with a completely different texture. The long, linear foliage ends up in a crest of smaller, linear leaflets. A small adjustment could be made in this case by separating the *Polystichum* and placing the *Asplenium* on the second shelf, between the two. These ferns can be swapped around easily as they are growing in pots. The plant at the top, *Blechnum spicant*, in its turn will form a pleasing contrast with the *Polystichum* if it is placed on the third tier.

The *Cotinus coggyria* in the image above is a great example of an oval-leaved plant and the combination with the grey foliage of the *Acacia baileyana* is excellent. The two plants form a strong contrast with each other because of the difference in the soft structure of the feathered leaf of the *Acacia* and the bold, oval structure of the *Cotinus* leaf – but they also complement each other as the purple-grey hue of the *Cotinus* is picked up by the grey leaf and purple leaf stalk of the *Acacia*. Combining plants that have some similarity in colour tends to be pleasing to the eye and forms a flow within the display. This can be as little as the colour of a small leaf stalk being similar to a tone in the leaf of another plant.

OPPOSITE—A fern wall with *Blechnum spicant* (top), *Asplenium scolopendrium* Ramomarginatum Group (middle) and *Polystichum* (bottom).

ABOVE—*Cotinus coggygria* 'Grace' and *Acacia baileyana*

Juxtapose three or more plants in a complementary grouping and things start to get really exciting. The combination of the three shade-loving plants (right) is quite stunning. The colours add to the effect, but it is the combination of leaf shapes that forms the base. The linear leaf of the beautiful *Hakonechloa* cuts through the lance-shaped leaf of *Persicaria*, which in its turn straddles the heart-shaped *Epimedium*. The similarities in colour of the *Persicaria* and *Epimedium* add to the perfect teaming. The *Epimedium* is evergreen and the *Hakonechloa* turns a golden wheat colour in winter, which ensures there is still a good contrast in foliage during the winter months.

The intricate combination below shows a group of plants which all have a different leaf shape. On looking closely, it becomes apparent that there is a theme running through them, which is the bronze colour. The theme starts with the mix of *Aeonium* with its dark tones, then the geranium has a leaf pattern with the same shade; running along towards the right is a sprig of bronze fennel and the lines in the *Persicaria* leaf at the back form the natural ending to the scheme. The leaf shapes go from oval to palmate, filigree to lance-shaped.

ABOVE—*Persicaria microcephala* 'Red Dragon', *Hakonechloa macra* 'Aureola' and *Epimedium x versicolor*.

LEFT—*Aeonium* (mixed), feathery *Foeniculum vulgare* 'Purpureum', *Geranium phaeum* var. *phaeum* 'Samobor' and *Persicaria runcinata* 'Purple Fantasy' (top right).

THE JUNGLE GARDEN

Striking combinations can be made when using plants originating from areas with the same growing conditions, and often these are the most effective combinations. Recreating the conditions of the original habitat, or finding plants which are suitable for the aspect of the garden, will see plants thrive and reach their full potential. The *Begonia luxurians*, *Podophyllum versipelle* 'Spotty Dotty' and *Matteuccia struthiopteris* pictured right all originate from damp and shady woodlands. They flourish in a shady area of this garden where humidity is high and the soil has been improved with organic matter such as leaf mould, which would be similar to the soils in their native habitat.

RIGHT—*Begonia luxurians* with *Matteuccia struthiopteris* (shuttle-cock fern) and *Podophyllum versipelle* 'Spotty Dotty'. The dark green, palmate leaf of the *Begonia* almost finds its opposite in the lime-green filigree leaf of the *Matteuccia* and the addition of *Podophyllum versipelle* 'Spotty Dotty' with its completely different shape and texture creates a successful combination. All three plants are shade loving and will thrive in moisture-retentive soils.

Achieving good foliage combinations means you might need to move plants around a few times. When I take some of my more tender plants out of their winter storage I usually place them out first in their containers, leave them in position until the following day or weekend, and then plant them out. Even with a cooling off period like this you can sometimes realize certain combinations don't work, perhaps because the leaf shapes are too similar to each other and need a refreshing contrast. This can be as simple as moving the plant along a bit so another plant can be placed in between. At other times, accidental plant combinations can be surprisingly perfect. The picture above shows just such a chance partnering as the tree canopy of the *Robinia* is usually well above the leaves of *Iresine*. However, the *Robinia* has suckered here, making shoots appear from the roots of the plant. This can sometimes happen with certain plants when the root system is disturbed by digging around it.

ABOVE—Suckers of *Robinia pseudoacacia*, with its feathered leaf, form a coincidental combination with the lance-shaped leaf of *Iresine herbstii* 'Aureoreticulata'.

OPPOSITE—Two begonias of extremes. The bold, heart-shaped leaf of *Begonia variegata* and the feathered leaves of *Begonia sutherlandii* 'Saunders Legacy'.

THE JUNGLE GARDEN

Sometimes combinations of the same leaf shape are possible if the detailing of the leaf is different. The combination pictured left shows a *Brunnera macrophylla* 'Jack Frost' and a Heuchera 'Chocolate Ruffles'. Although both leaves are heart-shaped, the ruffled edge of the *Heuchera* is enough to break the pattern. Further definition is achieved by the dull cast of the *Brunnera* leaf surface contrasting with the glossy leaves of the *Heuchera*. The combination also illustrates how effective contrasting foliage colour can be. The dark purple, almost black of the *Heuchera* sets off the white, lace-like leaf pattern of the *Brunnera* beautifully. Both are hardy perennials so it is a long lasting combination.

OPPOSITE—The frosted pattern of *Brunnera macrophylla* 'Jack Frost' combines well with the glossy, dark leaf of *Heuchera* 'Chocolate Ruffles'. Contrast in both leaf colour and leaf edge makes this a perfect combination.

ABOVE—*Manihot grahamii*, with its intricately shaped palmate leaves, forms a small shrub in a sunny, protected position. Here it is combined with *Platycladus orientalis* 'Franky Boy'. This small conifer has yellow, wiry shoots, which wind their way through larger-leaved plants nearby. Apart from the shapes and textures of both plants, the bluish hue of the *Manihot* and the yellowish tones of the *Platycladus* complement each other too.

Encouraging exploration

By offering plants with different shapes, sizes and textures your visitors will want to explore, eager to find out if there are more completely different plants further down the garden. Another way to encourage exploration is to create hidden corners. In a larger garden this could mean having an area of taller, denser planting that has a hidden corner behind it (it might also block a sight line), or a sweeping path that the visitor will follow to see what is around the next corner. These hidden corners need to contain an interesting specimen plant, plant combination or even a sculpture or water feature so that the visitor doesn't feel their exploration has been a waste of time; their curiosity needs to be satisfied so that the walk around the rest of the garden continues.

ABOVE AND OPPOSITE—Dense planting hides what is further down the path, prompting the visitor to explore the garden to see what lies beyond the edge of visibility. In this case the path opens up to an area with succulents and other drought-tolerant plants which is unlike any other part of the garden.

Creating depth in the garden

Hidden corners not only encourage curiosity, they also create a sense of depth, even when in reality there is hardly any depth at all in the garden. An opening in the planting which offers only darkness beyond gives the illusion of something else further down the garden and can make even small courtyard gardens feel more expansive. Layering plants is a good method of achieving this effect and if all you have is a small patio, this can be done by elevating plants at the back by putting them on an upturned pot or wooden crate. The effect of this dark corner is to resemble an area where a path once led but is now overgrown. Nevertheless, it needs to be carefully planned and well maintained, otherwise the plants will soon fill in the small clearing and just form a dense block. This can still look attractive but there will be no curiosity about what lies behind all the jungle plants.

Another way of creating depth in the garden is to use plants with different leaf colours. While plants with lighter foliage can brighten up dark corners, darker leaves can also be used effectively as they can create the illusion of something lying beyond this darkness. For example, try planting a clump of *Persicaria microcephala* 'Red Dragon' (see page 205) somewhere down the garden. When that area is explored more closely the pattern of dark burgundy colour on the lance-shaped leaf of the *Persicaria* gives extra visual interest. For a plant that is a bit taller but doesn't take up too much space in a small garden, *Sambucus nigra* f. *porphyrophylla* Black Tower ('Eiffel 1') is ideal (see page 150). Most elderflowers get to a very large size very quickly, but this cultivar forms a narrow but tall column with dark, almost black, feathered leaves. It would be perfect on the corner of a path, just hiding what is on the other side of it. On the other hand, corners in the deeper shade can be filled with plants with light foliage to give the illusion of the sun shining through the canopy of trees, hitting that particular spot. The effect will be one of space and openness.

LEFT—The darker areas to the right of the path foster the illusion of journeying into dense jungle. It makes the relatively narrow border appear to go on beyond what can be seen. These fathomless corners are created by dense planting of species with dark-coloured foliage.

OPPOSITE—Light-coloured plants such as *Iresine herbstii* 'Aureoreticulata', to the left of the path, brighten up a corner of the garden which has lower light levels.

OPPOSITE—A stream, with lots of shady and hidden corners bordering it, increases the perceived depth of the garden.

ABOVE—Dense vegetation, with climbers creating additional height, obscures the view of what lies beyond, making the jungle space appear to go on forever.

Jurassic

The term Jurassic refers to a 56-million-year-long period which ended 145 million years ago when dinosaurs still roamed the earth. In jungle gardening, however, it refers to a certain look of plants that are not always specific to that era. Jurassic plants have big, lush, green leaves, often with interesting textures. Planting a combination of them densely together will take you back a few million years and make you feel quite small... and perhaps a little apprehensive about what lies around the next corner.

plants

Two plants can't be left out when aiming for a Jurassic feel in the garden and these are *Tetrapanax papyrifer* 'Rex' (or T. 'Rex') and *Dicksonia antarctica*. Their massive leaves will quickly fill a space and when they grow taller they will form a beautiful upper canopy, providing shade and a feeling of immersion in the jungle. Although *Dicksonia* is slow growing it can be purchased as a half-standard or standard plant where the latter will usually have a trunk just under 2m (6½ft). Both these plants are readily available but another more unusual plant for upper canopy is *Schefflera macrophylla*. Macrophylla means large leaf and that is what you get. The large palmate leaf is divided into leaflets of great size. Its habit is quite open so light-loving plants will tolerate being planted underneath it.

ABOVE—*Dicksonia antarctica*

BELOW—*Schefflera macrophylla*

ABOVE—*Tetrapanax papyrifer* 'Rex'

LEFT—*Lobelia bambuseti* is not often seen in gardens but it provides a lot of impact. It is hard to imagine this plant is a close relative of the small blue- or white-flowering bedding plants we use in the garden as they are at opposite ends of the spectrum. Where the bedding plant has small flowers and very fine leaves, *Lobelia bambuseti* has massive leaves and can grow a flower spike 8m (26ft) tall. It is unusual for it to flower in colder climates but the large, lance-shaped leaves provide so much impact that they will not be missed.

Tall plants are important to give the sense of scale needed to create the Jurassic look, but densely planted understorey plants are equally important. The large leaves of these lower-level plants bring dense, full planting to the border and also create darker corners which enhance the sensation of never-ending expansiveness we associate with being in a Jurassic jungle before mankind arrived and began cutting paths and roads.

LEFT—A good plant for a Jurassic look is *Equisetum camtschatcense*, which will spread rapidly through the garden and send up stems which are green with black bands. These horsetails have a very long history and were among the first plants to colonize the earth, having been around for over 350 million years. Some giant species of horsetail which can grow up to 3 or 4m (10-13ft) are sometimes seen in botanical gardens. It may be best to grow this *Equisetum camtschatcense* in a pot or another contained area as it can be invasive. When grown in a pot it will need regular watering and should be placed on a saucer.

ABOVE—*Typhonium venosum* is a good understorey plant for a shady position. It has a very unusual leaf, and the spotted stems give extra impact. The leaves can easily grow to 40cm (16in) across and the leaflets together follow a half-moon shape.

CHAPTER 3

A Jungle Garden for Every Space

No matter what kind of outside space you have, there is always room to give it a jungle feel. The green and diverse foliage will create calmness and interest at the same time, and in hot gardens will enable a cooling effect. In exposed gardens, it will provide privacy and shelter, making the garden seem far removed from the rest of the world.

Sunny sites

In a natural jungle, many of the plants growing under the canopy of trees will be shade-loving species. However, a jungle garden is not just for people who have a shady and damp outside space; the effect can also be achieved with great success on a sunny site. The benefit of creating a jungle garden on such sites is that it can provide some shelter from harsh sun and there are many plants that will adapt to their environment, tolerating various levels of light. For instance, plants which have silvery, hairy foliage or thick, fleshy stems and leaves have evolved to survive in sunny, hot and dry conditions. Plants which have been grown in shadier spots may sometimes scorch in sunlight, but most will adapt to their new location and the following flush of leaves can be more tolerant of sun.

Of course, moisture in the soil is a factor here too. If plants that normally prefer shade are grown in sun, keeping them watered ensures they don't dry out too quickly and helps to keep the leaves cool. Even so, there are limits to this tolerance and plants which grow naturally in shady and boggy areas will not tolerate bright sunshine and dry conditions; those with thin, yellow or white-variegated leaves will often scorch in a sunny spot. Creating an upper canopy of taller plants with larger foliage means that the ground beneath will become more suitable for plants which can't tolerate too much sunshine. This upper canopy can also be helpful in areas that are often affected by frost as it will create a sheltered micro-climate. An exposed and sunny site can also be planted with a variety of succulent plants with their thick, fleshy stems or plants with a hairy leaf surface to create more of a dry jungle.

LEFT—*Geranium maderense*

OPPOSITE—Both the soft and silvery foliage of *Gazania* 'Bicton Orange' and the thick, fleshy leaves of *Aloe polyphylla* have adapted to withstand high levels of sunlight and low levels of moisture and humidity.

Best plants for dry and sunny gardens

- *Agave*
- *Aloiampelos striatula*
- *Cussonia paniculata*
- *Echium*
- *Ficus johannis* subsp. *afghanistanica*
- *Geranium maderense*
- *Ginkgo biloba*
- *Kniphofia northiae*
- *Melianthus major*
- *Neopanax laetus*

ABOVE—An upper canopy has been planted in this sunny garden to create shade underneath. Moisture levels will remain higher and a larger range of plants can be used because of the intentionally created shade.

ABOVE—An olive tree (*Olea europaea*) forms a focal point in this sunny garden.

Upper canopy

When choosing the larger plants which will provide dappled shade under their canopy, leaves are again the focus. Plants with a smaller leaf surface will evaporate less water and are better adjusted to drier conditions. A great example of this is *Albizia julibrissin*, whose very fine, feathered leaves form a canopy which will filter the light beautifully. The cultivar 'Summer Chocolate' has brown-purple leaves. It is certainly one to plant if you want to achieve *komorebi*, the Japanese name for the effect of scattered sunlight shining through leaves. *Albizia* will form a small tree which can be pruned easily, so is suitable for small- to medium-sized gardens.

If you have a bit more space, consider *Aralia elata* which, because of its thorny stems, is also called devil's walking stick. It is fast-growing and the feathered leaves will reach a large size quite quickly. The filtered light created by the canopy will mean you can grow plants that need full or dappled shade underneath.

For a truly impressive plant that casts shade try *Tetrapanax papyrifer* 'Rex' – even one of these in your garden will give the jungle effect. Some winter protection may be needed in colder climates, especially when the plant is younger, but it is certainly worth the effort. The huge palmate leaves appear very early in spring. This plant can grow to 3–4m (10–13 ft) high in a sunny, sheltered spot and will provide a great canopy which ensures the ground beneath stays shady and protected from the harshest sun. If your garden is too small to let the *Tetrapanax* grow freely, it is easily pollarded and pruned. Should the garden be too cold for a *Tetrapanax*, the alternative is the hardy palm *Trachycarpus fortunei*, which also has large leaves and forms a good canopy.

Another impressive upper-canopy plant is the hardy banana *Musa basjoo*. Although these plants can flower and fruit in our climate, the bananas, even in their native habitat, remain approximately 5cm (2in) long and are not very tasty at all; the inside is like a grainy gelatine without any banana flavour. The plant itself though is fast-growing and will form paddle-shaped leaves that are easily 1m (3¼ft) long and 40cm (16in) wide. The stems can reach 4–5m (13–16ft) in a sheltered spot, especially when they are protected with hessian and straw in areas with cold winters. The root system stays relatively small, so alternatively these plants could easily be dug up in autumn and overwintered indoors. If they do get affected by the frost in winter, the more mature plants will shoot up again from the base in most cases. The height of the stems will be lost, but in a sunny garden the banana can easily reach 1.5–2m (4–6 ½ft) in one growing season, still providing some shade for plants growing near it.

ABOVE—The fine, feathered leaf of *Albizia julibrissin* 'Summer Chocolate'.

OPPOSITE—Fast-growing plants such as *Musa basjoo*, *Dahlia imperialis* and *Eucalyptus glaucescens* form the upper canopy in this garden, sheltering shade-loving plants from the sun and providing protection against cold weather.

LEFT—Tetrapanax papyrifer 'Rex' with its very large leaves ensures the ground beneath stays shady and protected from the harshest sun.

BELOW—Creating a diverse upper canopy in a garden means a wider range of plants can be grown underneath. This diversity can exist in leaf shape and size, but also in density of the foliage. Where a *Tetrapanax* will provide deep shade under its canopy, the more open habit of upper canopy plants such as *Musa basjoo* (centre) and *Pseudopanax crassifolius* (right) won't shade the ground underneath too much, so plants which don't grow well in deep shade still get sufficient levels of sunlight.

Best upper canopy plants

- *Acacia pravissima*
- *Acer palmatum*
- *Albizia julibrissin*
- *Aralia bipinnata*
- *Dahlia imperialis*
- *Dicksonia antarctica*
- *Kalopanax septemlobus*
- *Musa basjoo*
- *Tetrapanax papyrifer* 'Rex'
- *Trachycarpus fortunei*

ABOVE— *Schefflera taiwaniana* filters the light. As the canopy isn't very dense, it provides good light-levels for a wide range of planting underneath.

RIGHT—For colder climates *Trachycarpus fortunei* (left of the chairs) can be used successfully as an upper canopy plant. Its canopy is more transparent than that of the *Tetrapanax papyrifer* 'Rex' on the right-hand side which, combined with its non-branching, upright stem, makes it suitable for narrower borders which don't want to be shaded out completely.

Planting in drier soils

The sunny jungle garden can be just as great as a shade garden and if the soil is drier it is usually possible to grow plants that are slightly more tender. This is because in many cases the frost doesn't kill plants: it's the wet soil that is detrimental to their chances of survival. Another advantage of a drier soil is that it takes less energy to heat up. This means that in spring plants will come up sooner and flower earlier than on soils which retain more water. At one of my places of work we had a tropical garden which had been mulched every year with compost. This meant that the soil level was raised gradually by about 30cm (12in), which in turn resulted in a well-drained border. The spring display of tulips in this garden was consistently two or three weeks ahead of those in other parts of the (much wetter) garden.

The same effect can be achieved by growing plants in pots, as apart from the drainage being much better than in a border, the sides of the pot will be heated up by the sun, providing warmth to the roots. Plants will come up earlier, but will also retain their foliage longer in autumn. In a garden which is drier this effect will appear naturally, although mulching drier gardens will be beneficial to your soil structure and moisture levels.

LEFT—Diversity of planting in a sunny and dry site with (*anti clockwise from right*): *Aloiampelos striatula, Ficus johannis* subsp. *afghanistanica, Agave salmiana* var. *ferox* and *Aeonium hierrense.*

ABOVE—Large specimen plants such as this *Agave americana* 'Variegata' stand out from the rest of the planting and give the necessary vertical lines. In their own way they form the upper canopy in this garden.

Although the garden at St Michael's Mount in the image above is in south-west England, where the prevailing westerly wind brings high rainfall, the plants still have to cope with dry conditions, due to the sloping nature of the terrain. If the plants weren't on this slope where water drains straightaway, some of these probably wouldn't survive the wet conditions. But the rocky ground underneath, as well as the porous substrate the plants are growing in, mean the root system doesn't stand in water, which would otherwise make it rot. In a garden, this kind of extreme drainage could be recreated by building up a border with hardcore or large rocks and laying an open substrate such as lava rock, in between which the plants can be placed.

LEFT—The spiky *Aloe ferox* forms a good contrast with the soft-textured *Aeonium canariense*.

ABOVE—The gardens at St Michael's Mount in Cornwall are on a cliff face. Despite the high amount of rainfall in this area, the plants grow in extremely well-drained conditions and need to be able to tolerate drought. Leaf textures as well as shapes and colours create a diverse planting. Succulent leaves and grey surfaces ensure evaporation of water is limited.

THE JUNGLE GARDEN

OPPOSITE AND ABOVE—
Succulents grown on well-draining pumice stone which allows them to tolerate lower temperatures in winter. With these plants, winter wet is often more of an issue for their survival than low temperatures. In the picture above, the spiral-shaped *Aloe polyphylla* (centre) and *Aeonium cuneatum are* underplanted with a green carpet of *Soleirolia soleirolii, which* softens the hard, rocky surface.

Succulents outside

Succulents are ideal plants for sunny, dry positions. They have adapted to survive in the hottest and driest conditions by forming thick, fleshy stems, often silvery in colour. Most of these plants will survive frosts in a well-drained position or when grown in a pot.

There are many succulents which are hardy, but to improve any of their chances of surviving the colder winters, drainage is very important. This can be achieved by adding rocks and gravel to a border and planting the succulents in this medium rather than in the existing soil underneath. When growing in pots the drainage can be improved by using a sandy compost mixture and adding a layer of gravel to the bottom of the pot before placing the compost on top. Broken terracotta pots are often used to improve drainage but take care because shards of this crockery can block the hole in the bottom of the pot, actually making drainage worse. Some succulents may not be suitable for keeping outside during winter, even when taking these extra measures of protection, so check their hardiness tolerance. The best place to overwinter them them is on a south- or west-facing windowsill, or in a garage or glasshouse. When overwintering in a garage or glasshouse the humidity levels cannot be too high as otherwise the plant will still rot. Avoid watering too often and make sure the soil dries out completely between watering.

Using succulents in the garden does not limit the options in terms of colour palette. Succulent foliage comes in a wide range of colours and it is important, when making combinations, to use an array of pronounced colours as otherwise, especially in bright and sunny conditions, the colours may look a bit flat. We have all seen houses in sunnier climes painted in colourful hues such as bright blue or green which have good impact under blue skies and the principle is the same with plants. By contrast, some *Aeonium*, such as the cultivar 'Zwartkop', have dark, almost black leaves and these will temper the brightness if needed and contrast well with silver-leaved plants, as will plants with yellow leaves such as *Sedum rupestre* 'Angelina' (seen at the centre of the image left).

OPPOSITE—A selection of *Aeonium*, *Sedum* and *Graptoveria* form a good combination as there is difference in leaf thickness as well as colour.

ABOVE—The drainage in this garden has been improved in order to grow a wide range of succulents all year round. The diversity in form, shape and height of the succulents provides interest and the space between each plant ensures these characteristics can be appreciated fully.

LEFT—*Agave filifera* is unusual because of the white threads along the leaf edge. In a well-drained position it is hardy to at least -15°C (5°F).

BELOW—*Aloe polyphylla* growing sideways on a wall. This ensures no water will get trapped in the crown, preventing rot in wetter seasons.

OPPOSITE—*Echinopsis terscheckii* needs a well-drained and sheltered position to survive outside in winter.

Dappled shade

Having a garden in dappled shade, or creating dappled shade yourself by introducing larger plants which will provide a canopy, opens up a whole range of extra possibilities for creating a jungle garden with a wide range of leaf shapes and textures. Plants such as bananas, *Tetrapanax papyrifer* 'Rex', bamboo, or small trees such as *Albizia* or *Robinia* can filter light in a sunny garden and create dappled shade. Sometimes, though, gardens can already have dappled shade because of trees growing next door. A situation like this is ideal for creating a dense jungle garden full of lush foliage; the filtered light means that plants which do not tolerate bright sunshine can thrive. As the garden still gets some sunshine, the range of suitable plants for these spaces is quite extensive. Creating dappled shade is beneficial for any jungle garden, as not only will shade-loving plants grow better under a canopy of taller shrubs or trees, there will be less evaporation of water in the garden beneath. The canopy of plants, especially when planted densely, can create a micro-climate as it shades the soil, meaning it will retain moisture better and for longer.

Gardens with some dappled shade can still be quite dry, as in parts the sun will still go through the canopy and heat up the air. To increase humidity, and create a better environment for large-leaved plants, the addition of a pond or a stream can make a big difference. Even using a butler's sink as a water feature can give extra interest. Water in the garden will give a cooling effect, increasing moisture levels and forming an ecosystem for all kinds of wildlife that like the damper surroundings. It adds greatly to the jungle effect and the overall atmosphere in the garden and will create the right environment for ferns, which love high humidity and hate getting too dry. Especially on hot summer days later in the year, the humidity can prevent the leaves from turning brown and crispy.

BELOW—The filigree leaves of *Dicksonia antarctica* on the right are contrasted beautifully by the round leaves of the water lily, *Nymphaea pygmaea*. An added attraction of water in the garden is the mirroring effect of the water surface. This can be enhanced by adding black dye to the water. As this dye is a food colourant it is perfectly safe for any wildlife in the pond.

THE JUNGLE GARDEN

LEFT—In this sunny garden, dappled shade has been created by planting large-leaved plants such as *Tetrapanax papyrifer* 'Rex' and *Dicksonia antarctica* (not pictured). This has created pockets of dappled shade in which shade-loving plants such as hosta and hakonechloa thrive. The white flowers of *Trachelospermum jasminoides* on the left-hand side produce a delightful scent which, because of the shelter of the upper canopy plants, lingers in the air.

BELOW—The small pond in this garden doesn't just provide higher levels of humidity for the planting around the edge, it also creates a good habitat for wildlife such as frogs, pond skaters and birds that will drink from it in hot summers.

Best plants for dappled shade

– *Aegopodium podagraria* 'Gold Marbled'
– *Acanthus mollis* 'Hollard's Gold'
– *Brassaiopsis mitis*
– *Colocasia esculenta* 'Pink China'
– *Equisetum* 'Bandit'
– *Eriobotrya japonica* 'Okân'
– *Plectranthus* 'Brunsendorf'
– *Rubus lineatus*
– *Sambucus nigra* 'Linearis'
– *Schefflera macrophylla*

OPPOSITE—Large trees behind the bench provide the garden with dappled shade. This area is too shady for a lawn so *Soleirolia soleirolii* (mind-your-own-business) is used as a lush, green, alternative groundcover. A narrow, wood chip path behind the bench leads into a more informal, dense jungle planting.

ABOVE—The thin, feathered leaves of *Albizia julibrissin* filter the light just enough for plants that like dappled shade to grow underneath.

Shade

A garden can be shady because of dense planting all around it, existing trees, or the position of the surrounding buildings in relation to it. Sometimes people struggle to find suitable plants when gardening in dense shade, but in natural jungles most plants grow under large trees which provide a lot of shade too. There are many hardy, shade-loving perennials with large leaves and these will grow well in gardens with low light levels. Often these gardens have more moisture in the ground as well as in the air because the sun is less powerful. High humidity levels are beneficial to plants with large leaves as their evaporation rate will be compensated for; they will retain their size and will not develop brown scorch marks. In these lower light levels variegated plants can give extra colour and can brighten up darker spots. Small woodland plants such as *Convallaria* have cultivars with striped or completely yellow leaves. *C. majalis* 'Albostriata' (see page 186), for instance, has yellow stripes along the linear leaves and 'Golden Jubilee' is a cultivar with completely yellow leaves. These plants provide a subtle source of brightness under plants with a denser canopy and can form a change in leaf shapes and patterns. Even if the planted area is only a darker corner on a patio or in a courtyard garden, the brighter leaves create light and a feeling of space.

Plants with leaves that have colours such as yellow and red provide warmth in shaded, cooler gardens. Subconsciously they are associated with fires, whereas the cooler-coloured plants with white variegation, for instance, suggest ice and snow. The range of shade-loving plants is quite extensive, but *Podophyllum* is among my favourites. These hardy plants have huge leaves, sometimes with a pattern of brown patches, and will only thrive in shade gardens as sunlight will scorch the leaves and make the patterns fade to green more quickly. Many of these shade-loving plants will produce even larger leaves when grown in deep shade as they are trying to capture as much light as possible for

the process of photosynthesis. A larger leaf surface means more chlorophyll and more opportunity to create energy to grow.

The image above shows a group of plants in deep shade. They are grown in pots to retain the patio underneath but also because they can be moved around easily. Some plants are at their best early in the year, when they are placed at the front, later to be swapped with plants at the back which are then at their best. In a situation like this, where space is limited, it can be quite difficult to get the balance of leaf shapes and textures right.

ABOVE—Shade-loving plants such as *Farfugium japonicum* 'Aureomaculatum' (left), *Brassaiopsis mitis (bottom right), Athyrium (centre)* and *Asplenium scolopendrium* (Crispum Group) 'Golden Queen' (bottom) will thrive in deep shade and do well in pots.

OPPOSITE—Plants with white variegation such as *Hosta undulata* var. *albomarginata* and *Glechoma hederacea* 'Variegata' (trailing plant to the left of the tree) can brighten up shady gardens.

Small courtyard gardens are often in shade for much of the day. Hostas are perfect for such areas as they love shade and can be grown in pots very successfully. They also retain their colour better in shadier spots as often too much sunshine can make variegation turn green, bleach the leaves or scorch them, making them turn brown and crispy. Hostas and ferns form a perfect combination as the light and airy filigree leaves of ferns contrast with the bold structure of the large-leaved, heart-shaped hosta leaf. Another great contrast with these large leaves are grasses, of which *Hakonechloa macra*, or Japanese forest grass, is one of the finest. The linear leaves of this grass are so light that even the slightest breeze will create movement in the clump. Although hostas do die down in late autumn, this is preceded by stunning colours of butter-yellow. The ferns and *Hakonechloa* turn a beautiful wheat colour and retain their foliage until they are cut down in early March, providing interest throughout winter.

Another good deciduous perennial for a shady courtyard is *Stachys byzantina* 'Big Ears', or lamb's ear, which has the most velvety-soft, grey oval leaves you can find – there aren't many people who won't walk up to this plant to feel its texture. Their leaves have soft hairs all over them and contrast well with smooth leaves providing added interest. *Stachys* prefers to grow in full sun but will still do well in shade, apart from not producing as many flowers. Some of the hostas have a similar bluish tint to the colour of the *Stachys*, which means that although the texture is very different, there is cohesion in the colour palette. The final recommendation for a shady courtyard mix is *Disporum longistylum* 'Night Heron'. This relative of Solomon's seal loves shade and when it emerges in spring the new stems and leaves come up in a very dark, almost black colour. Later in the year this fades to a dark green but often the edges of the leaves retain the darkness. The fine, lance-shaped leaves are a great contrast to the other bold structures and although they are sturdy, they add airiness to planting combinations. It provides this structure throughout winter and can be cut back in spring before the new shoots appear.

Best plants for shade

- *Aspidistra sichuanensis*
- *Athyrium filix-femina* 'Dre's Dagger'
- *Begonia luxurians*
- *Convallaria majalis* 'Albostriata'
- *Dryopteris wallichiana*
- *Farfugium japonicum* 'Aureomaculatum'
- *Hakonechloa macra* 'All Gold'
- *Ophiopogon japonicus*
- *Oplopanax horridus*
- *Podophyllum versipelle* 'Spotty Dotty'

THE JUNGLE GARDEN

ABOVE—Leaves of *Stachys byzantina* 'Big Ears' are soft like velvet.

OPPOSITE—Here pots contain a combination of *Hosta*, *Hakonechloa macra (left)*, *Polystichum setiferum (right)* and *Disporum longistylum* 'Night Heron' *(centre)*.

ABOVE—This border in a shady area of the garden shows great diversity in its planting scheme. The yellow grass *Hakonechloa macra* 'Aureola' surrounded by ferns such as *Osmanthus regalis* (top), *Dryopteris wallichiana* (centre) and the orange *Dryopteris erythrosora* 'Brilliance' (centre right) show different leaf forms, whilst *Persicaria microcephala* 'Red Dragon' (bottom right) adds a contrasting colour.

CHAPTER 4

Jungle Perfection

Achieving jungle perfection can be a gradual process. People may start by liking a certain type of plant and as they become more interested in it expand on the theme. Inspiration can be found all across the world in public gardens but often the best examples of jungle planting can be found in other people's private gardens. Seeing what plant combinations work for others in a range of different conditions is an important part of creating your own jungle garden.

JUNGLE LIVING

This inviting garden is a great example of how to achieve the jungle look around spaces for relaxation and entertaining. The patio area feels like a clearing in the undergrowth and the boundary planting makes it seem as if the jungle stretches into the distance.

Bold structures and big leaves prevent the visitor from being able to see what is beyond, triggering the imagination to believe there is a jungle that cannot be seen. Taller plants which slightly overhang the open area create the feeling of being immersed in dense vegetation. A dominant feature is the beautiful *Tetrapanax papyrifer* 'Rex' which is of a size that means it hangs over the garden and its massive leaves can be viewed from underneath. The bold structure of the palmate leaves is set off well against the sky but also forms a good combination with the pink-variegated, linear leaves of the *Phormium* beneath it. This colour adds interest as do the brown, felty stems of the *Tetrapanax* which add extra interest to this already magnificent plant.

The canopy of the *Tetrapanax* over the garden gives a sense of immersion in the greenery and the sunlight which filters through the leaves provides shade for the plants below as well as the occupants of the deck chairs. The palmate shape of the *Tetrapanax* leaves is mirrored on the other side of the garden by a *Trachycarpus fortunei*. This hardy palm has a more upright habit and glossier leaves

than the *Tetrapanax* which provides a subtle contrast. Further in the garden this particular leaf shape is repeated again by *Fatsia japonica* 'Tsumugi-shibori', ensuring a pattern and repetition in the garden, but the colour of the leaf, which is white-spotted, stands out against the other leaves. This particular plant is flanked by the arum lily *Zantedeschia aethiopica* 'Crowborough', its heart-shaped leaves making a good contrast with the *Fatsia* leaf and in this case even the serrated edge which was caused by vine weevil forms a different texture and has its own attractiveness.

A plant with a bold structure that is used on the boundary of this garden is *Paulownia tomentosa*. When it isn't pruned it will turn into a large, quite fragile tree, but here it is coppiced every year to make it produce its large leaves and tall stems. Behind it is a fig which has a palmate leaf and contrasts very well with the large, heart-shaped leaves of the Paulownia. Once established, both plants are good growers and will produce a lot of foliage. The fig can be trained along the boundary to form a dense barrier which enforces the feeling of being in a jungle clearing.

OPPOSITE—Boundary planting with *Tetrapanax papyrifer* 'Rex' (right) and *Trachycarpus fortunei* (left) providing the upper canopy.

BELOW LEFT—Coppiced *Paulownia tomentosa* can grow 4 to 5m (13–16ft) in one year. Because of the fast growth it will form straight shoots without side branches so is ideal as a narrow screen on the boundary of the garden.

BELOW RIGHT—*Fatsia japonica* 'Tsumugi-shibori' (right) with *Zantedeschia aethiopica* 'Crowborough'.

THE JUNGLE GARDEN

Further towards the house is an outdoor dining space which benefits from the overhanging planting in the garden, but because the planting there has lighter structures and textures, there is a feeling of space. The most prominent leaf colour in this area comes from the trained copper beech. The round, dark leaves are set off by the light wall behind it, but also by the blue-grey *Festuca glauca* in the pot in front of it. The dark colour of the beech accentuates the structure of the plant and its leaves and the light grass in the front softens that effect.

OPPOSITE—Narrow, linear leaves of the silvery *Astelia chathamica* and the blue grass *Festuca glauca* gracefully fall over the decking, softening the edges of the seating area. All form a fine contrast with the large leaves of the *Tetrapanax papyrifer* 'Rex' overhead.

ABOVE—Lush, green tabletop plants spill out of their containers so one is surrounded by green even while dining.

THE CONTEMPORARY JUNGLE GARDEN

A jungle effect can be achieved with just a small range
of plants. This structured planting, in patterns,
gives a very minimalistic look, but the diversity in leaf
shapes and textures still draws in the eye and encourages
exploration of the garden.

The lush, green ferns (*Dryopteris wallichiana*) with their dark stems give the garden a Jurassic feel, despite being planted at wide intervals. This particular fern comes up with brown fronds in spring and shows perfect crosiers, giving the garden a totally different look at that time of year.

In this garden the existing design feature of the front wall is reflected in the squares of clipped box and the square paving slabs. The colour of the slabs and the gravel is very similar, giving the whole garden coherence and forming a contrast with the shades of green of the plants. The pattern of blocks and square corners in this garden is carried on in the arrangement of the ferns, which are planted in large rectangles. Although they give the garden a looseness with their filigree leaves which splay around randomly, they are spaced out evenly.

Another feature in the garden which softens the hard edges is the small tree (*Crataegus*) by the wall. The height is perfect as it blocks out most of the neighbouring houses, without the patterns and spacious feeling of the rest of the garden being compromised, and provides some shade for the ferns in the garden. Spaciousness in this garden is also achieved by the colour of the fence. This is a dark colour with shrubs (*Magnolia grandiflora*) planted in front of it. The combination gives the appearance of the shrubs being at the front of dense planting, where the darkness prevents seeing exactly what is beyond.

OPPOSITE—Minimalistic and formal planting creates a different kind of jungle look, a formalized version of the jungles we see in nature.

BELOW—*Dryopteris wallichiana*

RIGHT—Evenly spaced
Dryopteris wallichiana give
formality but their loose habit
softens the edges.

THE GARDEN ROOM

When gardens are an extension of the indoor
living space and both spaces flow into each other
as if they were one, both are enhanced and seem
larger than they are in reality.

In this garden there are no barriers between the built extension and the outside patio (opposite). The only noticeable difference is the floor covering, which is wood indoors and a hard surface outdoors. In this design the link between inside and out has been carefully considered. The group of plants on the left is mirrored with a prominent group just inside the garden. Special attention has been paid to the habit of the plants. While those indoors are in a glass extension of the house and therefore need to be tolerant of hotter and drier air than the exterior plants, the arching habit of the *Howea foresteriana* (top left) matches that of the *Musa basjoo* outside. The same can be said for the linear leaf of the *Beaucarnea recurvata* indoors in the white pot and the *Furcraea longaeva* opposite beneath the *Musa*.

One of the main specimen plants in the garden is the *Musa basjoo*. The arching leaves form a perfect upper canopy, without becoming too dense. This, together with the other tall plants around the boundary, gives a feeling of having cover and privacy which is beneficial for relaxation. What it also does is frame the garden from the living space indoors, forming a focal point and a green, subtle division between the indoor and outdoor spaces.

OPPOSITE—The garden room forms an extension of the inside space, with similar plants connecting both areas.

LEFT—Exposing the stems of the *Phyllostachys aurea* gives the *Dicksonia antarctica* a chance to weave through. The filigree leaf is in stark contrast with the rigid bamboo stems.

ABOVE—*Musa basjoo* frames the garden and forms a subtle mark of where the indoor space ends and the outdoor space begins.

THE JUNGLE GARDEN

The garden has perfect combinations of leaf shapes and sizes, which is important as a lot of them are very similar in colour. It demonstrates how using just greens can still give a very interesting garden due to the differences in foliage type. The retaining wall at the end of the garden as well as the fence behind the bamboo are dark in colour, giving an illusion of depth. The side shoots of the bamboo (*Phyllostachys aurea*) have been thinned out to the height of the fence, ensuring a sense of space exists; if the bamboo were not pruned like this the garden would feel claustrophobic. The ability to see through the stems but encountering darkness beyond is a perfect way of boundary planting in a smaller garden as it creates the illusion of there being something more than the eye can see. The dark colour of the fence also contrasts with the bamboo stems, emphasizing their yellow-green colour.

In small gardens such as this one it is good practice to have certain leaf textures and shapes repeated, for if everything is different the effect can be messy, making the area seem smaller. Repetition in this garden is achieved with the linear leaves of *Furcraea longaeva* and *Agapanthus africanus* on the right-hand side and the two *Dicksonia antarctica* at the back. The feathered foliage of the *Albizia julbrussin* just inside the garden has almost the same texture as the tree ferns, which subtly enhances the appearance of repetition.

Using large specimen plants in a small garden gives it an almost instant jungle look. If this garden were to have just the bamboo, tree ferns and banana in it, it would still succeed in this respect. Often people with small gardens are afraid to plant large specimens as they feel the garden will feel cramped and claustrophobic. However, using large plants has great impact and makes the garden feel more relaxed than it would if it contained many different small plants.

OPPOSITE—The crown of the bamboo has been raised to the top of the fence, allowing its dark colour to create shadowy depths that make the garden appear bigger than it really is.

BELOW—*Furcraea longaeva*

THE POTTED JUNGLE

In this small city garden all the plants are grown in pots and the emphasis is entirely on having a good display of foliage throughout the year. It is easy to swap the plants around if some are looking particularly nice, warranting a place at the front.

To have colour all year around, a wide range of variegated leaves have been used. The sheltered position of the garden provides a micro-climate in which very tender plants can survive.

Growing plants in pots has more benefits than just being able to move them around. Plants which otherwise may spread too much through the garden can easily be contained when grown in pots. Also the diversity of planting can be greater. As potted plants all grow in their own growing medium, the compost, or additives can be specifically catered to each individual plant. This means plants which prefer ericaceous soil can be grown right next to plants which like the soil to be more neutral or alkaline. The same can be applied to moisture and drainage needs. It makes for an interesting garden in many ways not least because the individual needs of each plant provide extra horticultural involvement for the person looking after them.

A clever use of colour is evident in this garden, where subtle variegated lines are repeated throughout the planting arrangement. The group of plants in the image opposite, with *Cordyline australis* 'Torbay Dazzler' in the white urn as the centre point, shows this repetition very well. The *Convallaria majalis* 'Vic Pawlowski's Gold' (front, second from left) has a variegated stripe in the same tone as the *Cordyline* and this is again repeated in the *Ophiopogon japonicus* 'Nanus Variegatus' (on the ground, left of the zinc planter). The linear leaves of these three plants provide a good contrast with the large, bold and colourful leaves of the *Begonia rex* left of the zinc planter.

Further foliar colour combinations are pictured right with pink and grey variegated plants. The *Begonia rex* (left), *Tradescantia fluminensis* 'Nanouk' (top right) and *Agave parryi* (bottom right) form a good combination because of their shared tones of pink and grey, with the bold variegation of the begonia and the more linear variegation of the tradescantia creating a different pattern which in turn is a good contrast and creates interest. Teaming similar colours in a plant group makes the coherence stronger and is pleasing

to the eye. Here the grey of the agave is picked up by the grey of the begonia as well as the tradescantia and even the thorns on the agave reflect some of the pink colours of the other plants. Even the tiniest parts of plants can make a difference to how the border works.

OPPOSITE—Coloured leaves such as those of the *Begonia rex* are framed by green linear foliage, making them stand out further.

BELOW—Grey and pink tones link together the *Begonia rex* (left), *Tradescantia fluminensis* 'Nanouk' (top) and *Agave parryi*.

TOP LEFT—The variegated *Arthropodium candidum* 'Little Lilia' (centre) has a completely different leaf shape and texture to the surrounding plants. This, along with its bright variegation, makes it a focal point within the border.

BOTTOM LEFT—Variegated plants *Cordyline australis* 'Torbay Dazzler' (left) and *Reynoutria japonica* var. *compacta* 'Variegata' (right) are separated by plain green plants such as the *Metasequoia glyptostroboides* (foreground) so the variegation of each individual plant can be appreciated and patterns don't clash or merge into each other.

OPPOSITE—Creating different levels by placing some plants on columns or upturned pots gives the border depth without having to buy large plants. Pot displays are easy to move around or replace.

THE JUNGLE GARDEN

OPPOSITE—Colourful leaves form an important part of the design of this garden. In a shady garden such as this strong colours can provide a real lift.

LEFT—The sharp spikes on the edges of the leaf of *Epimedium* 'Spine Tingler' on the bottom right combine well with the softer edges of the variegated *Ophiopogon jaburan* 'Vittatus' and the *Soleirolia soleirolii* beneath it in the urn.

BELOW—Similar colours link in a diagonal pattern; the yellow variegation of the clivia at the bottom are picked up by the cordyline in the urn and the silver tones of the podocarpus in the centre are reflected in the echeveria seen as underplanting for the cordyline.

THE SHADY JUNGLE

The array of foliage shapes used in this garden makes it
a very interesting space. Although the path through the centre
is dominant, it is softened by plants around the edges. The path
provides good access to the back of the garden and the patio
at the end is just a widening of the hard landscaping rather
than a separate entity.

This gives the garden a good flow and invites the visitor to wander further down to explore several features in the garden. From the house the eye is drawn to the unusual shape and colours of *Podophyllum versipelle* 'Spotty Dotty' which, with its lime-green colour, is the same tone as the ferns opposite. The eye will go from left to right and the fine texture of the ferns invites people to approach to examine their intricacy. This curiosity is rewarded by finding a pond behind the ferns, containing interesting plants as well as wildlife. It cannot easily be seen from the house, so the reward of finding it hidden behind some plants makes the visitor want to see what is around the other corners of the garden.

The pond is shaded by plants overhead, making this an area of high humidity and giving it a cooling effect, which is perfect for the ferns and other plants around the edges. The overhead planting creates darker corners, which gives the area a sense of mystery as the visitor cannot quite see what lies beyond. This effect is emphasized by the use of the dark-leaved *Loropetalum chinense* var. *rubrum* 'Fire Dance'.

Another feature which subconsciously invites exploration is the upright willow screens. The frames the willows are placed in have been painted in a dark colour, making them almost invisible as they blend in with the shaded areas around the garden. Despite being of a natural material, the dark frames and straight lines of the willow within them give the garden a contemporary feel. Because the willow frames aren't solid they don't block out a lot of light, ensuring the garden feels spacious and giving the sense of looking through vegetation into a different part of the jungle; had they been solid structures the garden would feel far more dense and compact. The feeling of privacy comes from the larger plants around the edges of the garden.

The blocks of foliage from plants which have had their crowns lifted enhance the sense of the garden being divided in different spaces. Extra interest is added by keeping the willow screens narrow, as this creates another view into a different part of the garden to the side of the panels. These different angles of viewing make the garden seem larger and wider. If the only view were along the path, the area would be less interesting.

OPPOSITE—A shady garden with mainly hardy plants achieves a diverse and lush effect. The lime green colour of *Podophyllum versipelle* 'Spotty Dotty' in the foreground to the left of the path is reflected in the fern *Cyrtomium fortunei*, which is gracefully hanging over the path directly opposite. Clumps of the nearly black grass-like *Ophiopogon planiscapus* 'Nigrescens' are dotted along the length of the path and form a good contrast with leaf shapes and colours around them. Their colour is repeated in the dark red leaves of *Loropetalum chinense* var. *rubrum* 'Fire Dance' on the right-hand side of the image.

ABOVE—A pond hidden from the initial view encourages the visitor to explore more of the garden to discover if there are other hidden surprises.

THE JUNGLE GARDEN

While the willow panels frame areas of interest, their other function is to hide parts from view. The visitor to the garden will want to see what lies behind them, and it is important to have some kind of reward once the space becomes visible. In one of the areas behind a willow panel in this garden the point of interest is a *Pseudopanax ferox*. This architectural plant is from New Zealand and hardy to -10°C (14°F). Because of its open and narrow habit it can be planted at the front of the border where people will be able to touch the hard, linear leaves, which are serrated on the edges. Their brown colour adds to the slightly alien appearance of *Pseudopanax ferox*. An interesting and unusual plant such as this is precisely what is needed in hidden corners to encourage further exploration of the garden.

The planting within the borders of this garden has been done very well; there are good combinations of shade-loving plants which all have a distinct leaf shape, colour or texture. A good example is the border on the left-hand side of the path. The front is dominated by a *Podophyllum versipelle* 'Spotty Dotty', a perennial plant that has lobed, round leaves with dark spots. Behind it, *Mahonia eurybracteata* subsp. *ganpinensis* 'Soft Caress' has fine, linear leaves which are a good contrast with those of the *Podophyllum*.

This small shrub is evergreen and will provide structure and interest in winter. The palmate leaf of *Begonia luxurians* with the linear leaves of *Astelia chathamica* and *Epimedium latisepalum* provide three other shapes and textures, making this small border very diverse and interesting.

Throughout the garden, *Selaginella kraussiana* has been used as underplanting. It forms a carpet and resembles a mossy jungle floor, giving the garden a very natural and mature feel. Using a plant like this in a shade garden is very effective because it gives the lush, green, jungle look without the need to add many more plants.

OPPOSITE—Willow screens divide the garden into different sections and emphasize the vertical lines.

LEFT—This is an effective combination of shade-loving plants with distinct leaf shapes. *Selaginella kraussiana* forms the mossy base of the border.

ABOVE—Corners hidden by willow panels have interesting specimen plants to reward the visitor's curiosity and make them want to explore further.

THE ARID JUNGLE

This garden in south-east England is a fine example of how to create a jungle garden in a sunny, dry spot. Here the owner has worked with the elements rather than battling against them, using plants which can tolerate drought and a lot of sunshine.

For cacti to survive colder winters they need to be well drained and air has to flow around them, ensuring moisture moves away as quickly as possible. Here the garden owner has achieved this by adding a lot of lava rock to the garden and planting on a slope. Colder air is heavier than warm air so it will sink to the lower point in the garden, creating the air flow.

A *Phoenix canariensis* palm tree as well as *Trachycarpus*, *Yucca* and *Cordyline* add height to the garden at the upper canopy and mid-range level, while *Dasylirion*, *Agave* and *Phormium* create the understorey carpet of lower planting. By virtue of this tiered planting method the garden contains the diversity it needs to become exciting as it takes the visitor's view left and right, up and down. The emphasis here is on textures rather than foliage shapes. There is great contrast in the fleshy leaves of the succulents and the thin and narrow leaves of the taller plants such as the *Yucca* and *Phoenix* palm. In a sunny garden, the blue and silver colours of agave and the olive tree can also trick the mind into thinking the garden isn't as hot as it is in reality; the icy colours instead of bright reds and yellows, for instance, give a sense of cooler temperatures as they are associated with cold climates. The colours are in fact a protection for the plant as they reflect the harshest sunrays.

Another contrasting plant group within the garden are the cacti, which form spiky mounds. The vicious thorns on these plants are the opposite of the fleshy and cushion-like succulents which are planted among them. While the texture is more important than the shape, the globular form of the cacti does enhance the variety of shapes in a way that is completely different to other jungle gardens.

OPPOSITE—This scheme shows high, intermediate and low-level planting.

BELOW—Here fleshy, succulent leaves contrast with thin and narrow foliage.

ABOVE—The vertical lines of sun-loving *Echium pininana* (right) and *Echinopsis terscheckii* (left) draw the eye upwards. The large plants create the feeling of walking among giant jungle vegetation.

LEFT—On this sunny and dry site the spiky texture of the cacti is set off by the succulent, cushiony leaves of *Echeveria derenbergii*.

OPPOSITE—Despite the leaves all appearing linear, their different textures, thicknesses and colours give this border a great amount of interest.

THE JUNGLE GARDEN

LEFT—Good drainage due to the lava rock and gravel growing medium and the gradient of the garden ensure tender succulents can survive the cold, wet season.

THE BOTANICAL
JUNGLE

This garden belongs to a plant collector who loves to grow species with large, bold foliage. Plants dominate the space and when sitting on the patio, it's as if a space has been cleared in the jungle to allow for a few chairs.

Along the edge of the patio is a densely planted group of large plants which shows how effective a border can be when the convention of starting with small plants and gradually increasing in size towards the back of the border, is not followed. The large plants here form a barrier which prevents further views of the garden, enhancing the sensation of the open patio area just being hacked out in the jungle. The diversity of leaf shapes and textures along the patio give anyone who is relaxing in that area plenty to look at and it will be hard to resist exploring further.

From the patio, a red arch signals the entrance into the rest of the garden. Bright colours like this can be very effective in a predominantly green oasis; the red stands out and forms a very clear demarcation. The path meanders through the garden and around the only border which can be seen from the arch. This path is an invitation, but also leads the visitor to where they are intended to go next. The loop forms a logical route through the garden and takes you to further open spaces, a jungle lodge and misty glasshouses which contain special plants in this collection. Once the other spaces have been reached, the house cannot be seen and it feels as if you have been on a long expedition through the jungle.

OPPOSITE—Looking into the garden from the house, the large plants at the front of the border form a barrier which creates the impression of a dense jungle beyond.

BELOW—Plants in pots positioned closely together form a dense planting which screens further views of the garden. As the plants grow they can be moved around easily if needed.

LEFT—Red arches in this garden mark points of interest and lead the visitor in the desired direction.

OPPOSITE—Combinations of leaf shapes such as the serrated, linear leaf of *Sonchus acaulis,* the filigree *Dicksonia antarctica,* the heart-shaped *Podachaenium eminens* and the spiky *Solanum atropurpureum* give the interest and diversity that you would expect to find in a jungle.

THE JUNGLE GARDEN

A second red feature in the garden is the pergola. This gives the opportunity to grow unusual climbers and hides the garage which forms the garden border. The planting around the first red arch makes the visitor walking through it realize subconsciously that red garden features mean interesting plant species, so it will give anyone the urge to see what is around the next structure. This effect isn't achieved just with very obvious and colourful structures – it is also done with subtle points of various plants, which will lead the visitor from one of these points to the next, without realizing they are being led.

The planting throughout the garden is densely packed and layered very well, with a clear upper canopy of tall palm trees and tree ferns. This provides the necessary height and gives protection to lower-level plants which may not be entirely hardy. In a small way the large plants are creating a micro-climate where only slight fluctuations in temperature and humidity occur.

The colours in this garden are mainly shades of green. The leaf forms ensure that variety provides interest, but within the plants are subtle colours that provide coherence to the border. This makes the garden flow better and prevents the planting looking disunited. Many of the plants have dark red colouration, for example the leaf of *Ensete ventricosum* 'Maurelii', the stem of *Trachycarpus fortunei* and the leaf stalks of the *Schefflera* species. These thoughtful combinations break up the greenery very effectively.

OPPOSITE—Single representatives of interesting species are placed next to red landscaping features which pique the visitor's interest and set expectations for the remainder of the garden.

ABOVE—Subtle differences in shades of green bring the colour scheme of this garden alive. The glossy leaf of *Schefflera delavayi* stands out from the *Dicksonia antarctica* behind it which has a far more matt surface. The red petioles of the *Schefflera* form a further subtle contrast which only becomes apparent up close.

THE JUNGLE GARDEN

OPPOSITE—Taller plants provide a sheltering canopy for less hardy plants at lower levels. The dark red colour within some of the plants, such as the petioles on *Schefflera macrophylla* (centre front), gives the border coherence.

ABOVE—Another clearing in the jungle garden is surrounded by large plants such as *Dicksonia antarctica* (right) and *Trachycarpus fortunei (left)*. Because the open space is larger it is important to have these taller plants spreading over it so that the feeling of being immersed in the jungle isn't lost.

A CITY OASIS

This inner-city garden is surrounded by houses (and often construction works), but when you visit the garden none of the surrounding buildings or noise are apparent. A mature upper canopy blocks out the distractions and you are immersed in a tranquil green oasis.

A large *Robinia pseudoacacia* 'Frisia' has been placed at the end of the garden and elsewhere *Dicksonia antarctica* and *Tetrapanax papyrifer* 'Rex' have been used. At the lower level, bold architectural plants are to be found. The garden owner has not been afraid to use large plants in a relatively narrow space; the *Gunnera maculata* next to the tree fern can form leaves which are over 1m (3¼ft across. Although it is a herbaceous perennial, it will form part of the middle and upper canopy to give a true Jurassic jungle feel.

A straight path divides this garden in two. The surrounding plants soften the edges of its square slabs and ensure the straight lines are no distraction from the jungle feel. Along the path, a mix of evergreens and perennials has been used so that even in winter the path is broken up by loose planting. The colour yellow can be seen in the *Choisya ternata* 'Sundance' and *Hakonechloa macra* 'Aureola', with *Hosta* 'Sum and Substance' at the end of the path. This repetition of colours links the front of the path to the back and connects the two parts of the garden. The dark banana plant *Ensete ventricosum* 'Maurelii' is shown off by the lighter colours around it and forms a good focal point at the end of the path. An open clearing with a table and chairs just beyond what the eye can see becomes a reward for exploring the garden and a point from which the garden can be taken in. Lighter colours such as the yellow foliage of *Catalpa bignonioides* 'Aurea' are used along the edge here, emphasizing the feeling of openness and making the small space feel less claustrophobic. If darker foliage had been used, the space would feel more oppressive.

OPPOSITE—Creating a green oasis drowns out noise and hides buildings.

ABOVE—This bench looks as if it is swallowed up by jungle plants, an effect created by planting *Hakonechloa macra* 'Aureola' under the seat and a *Petasites japonicus* ssp. *giganteus* to the left of the bench. A potted *Chamaerops humilis* to the right of the bench completes the sense of enclosure.

LEFT—*Tetrapanax papyrifer* 'Rex', forming part of the upper canopy, is a plant that doesn't take long to establish but will need some frost protection in its early years. The hosta and ferns around the base of it enjoy the shade it casts while the tall bamboo (*Arundo donax*) to the right of the *Tetrapanax* weaves its way through the canopy to enjoy the sunshine above. The linear foliage of the bamboo combines well with the large, palmate leaves.

OPPOSITE—Dense planting along the straight path softens the edges and contributes to the jungle theme tremendously. Although small plants tend to be planted along paths, here the designer has used large leaves which give visitors the illusion of having to fight their way through dense vegetation. The white-flowering *Zantedeschia aethiopica* 'Crowborough' on the left, the red *Ensete ventricosum* 'Maurelii' behind it and the lime green *Hosta* 'Sum and Substance' underneath all add to this effect. The soft, yellow leaves of *Hakonechloa macra* 'Aureola' in the pot at the end provide a soft contrast to the large leaves and create movement in the garden at even the slightest breeze.

THE JUNGLE GARDEN

OPPOSITE—A small path leads through the garden, surrounded by large-leaved plants such as *Tetrapanax papyrifer* 'Rex' (right) and *Colocasia esculenta* (bottom). The dark-leaved cultivar *C. e.* 'Black Coral' to the left stands out for its colour and this dark burgundy shade is picked up behind by the dark, lance-shaped leaves of *Prunus cerasifera* 'Nigra'. Further down the path, *Trachelospermum jasminoides* grows over an arch. The sweet smell of its white flowers will linger in this densely planted and sheltered area.

ABOVE—An open space within the oasis where more vibrant colours are used contributes to the feeling of being in a bright clearing in the jungle.

LEFT—The yellow *Choisya ternata* 'Sundance' and *Chamaerops humilis* form a good combination of leaf shape and colour. The *Choisya* is allowed to weave itself through the palm, giving it a more natural and less orchestrated feel.

LUSH AND
LEAFY JUNGLE

If your garden is sunny, your range of jungle plants is not
limited to succulents and thick-leaved species; with soil
improvement and dense planting you can create the right
conditions to grow lush, leafy jungle plants too.

The largest part of my own jungle garden receives sunshine all day in summer and yet I hardly ever water it except for new plantings as the rootballs cannot yet soak up enough moisture from the ground. Once every three years I add a soil improver to my garden. I use coconut coir, but if your garden has poor soil quality you could use farmyard manure instead, or homemade leaf mould would be a good (and free) alternative.

The living room faces onto the back garden, with big windows all along the back of the house. When the weather is too poor to go outside there is still a good view of a diverse range of plants, for the garden is very much planted to face the house, as well as to provide a screen for buildings around the garden.

The patio is very straight and rectangular, so to soften it I have placed green and bright red pots all around the edges. The latter stand out and give extra colour to the garden throughout the year. I have only used two colours, for if many different-coloured pots are included then the overall look can become very messy – a jungle garden should be about the plants, not about the pots. Some of my plants that need more moisture are placed on saucers.

OPPOSITE—A view from the living room shows interesting plants facing the house. Even on rainy days the garden provides enough to look at from indoors.

BELOW—Plants in pots soften the edges of the patio. Any plants that have gone over are placed further to the back.

The rest of the garden is very straight, and quite narrow too. The garden space beyond the patio is a rectangle 5m (16ft) wide and 8m (26ft) long, with a narrow path leading straight to the back gate. To create the jungle feel in this small space, I have planted densely along the path. I don't mind the path being hidden and almost inaccessible, as it enhances the sensation of having to almost machete your way through dense jungle vegetation. The plants are interesting and unusual, as the visitor to the garden needs to be thrilled to have made the effort to see the diverse planting along the path. Tall plants line it and screen the garden wall, with *Catalpa* x *erubescens* 'Purpurea' towering above them all and marking a point where the path turns slightly to the right. This tree is coppiced to 30cm (12in) above ground every spring but will still grow to 3m (10ft) or more in summer.

LEFT—Dense planting with different leaf patterns such as *Manihot grahamii (centre left), Solanum betaceum (top left)* and *Platycladus orientalis* 'Franky Boy' (bottom left) provide plenty of visual interest for the visitor wandering down the path.

ABOVE—The layering of the garden is topped by the dark-leaved *Sambucus nigra* f. *porphyrophylla* Black Tower ('Eiffel 1'). This fast-growing plant provides height and shelter quickly. Once the *Tetrapanax* just beneath it has become tall enough to serve as upper canopy, the *Sambucus* will be cut down harder each year.

The upper canopy within the rest of the garden is provided by a fastigiate dark *Sambucus*. This is *Sambucus nigra* f. *porphyrophylla* Black Tower ('Eiffel 1'), which doesn't mind being in full sunshine. The dark colour tempers the bright sunlight in the garden and the height of the plant provides shade for those less fond of direct sunlight. *Sambucus* can be cut back very hard as it will soon shoot out to great heights again. Here it is cut back to about 1.2m (4ft) from the ground so not too much height is lost. Ultimately the *Tetrapanax papyrifer* 'Rex' will grow taller and can become the upper canopy of the garden. When that happens the *Sambucus* will be cut down further in spring. Fast-growing plants such as *Sambucus* can provide quick height and shelter in a garden while other plants are still to reach the desired height.

ABOVE—The mix of different leaf shapes is a theme in this garden. Even in the smallest space a high amount of diversity can be achieved. Silver tones of *Tradescantia zebrina* (centre front) are picked up by the tiny leaves of *Fuchsia microphylla* subsp. *hemsleyana* 'Silver Lining' directly to its right and the tall stems of *Amicia zygomeris* above right of it.

THE JUNGLE GARDEN

Although the focus of the garden is orientated to the living room, the path through it does lead to further interesting plants and a view across the garden. These different viewpoints are important in a small garden as it encourages walking back through it again and again, trying to spot something new every time. At the back of the garden is a small clearing where the visitor can get closer to the plants. Finer leaf textures are used here as they can be observed up close. The plants which stand out at this end because of their different textures and colours are *Rhus typhina* Tiger Eyes ('Bailtiger') and *Solanum atropurpureum*. The *Rhus* has yellow, velvety, feathered leaves whereas the *Solanum* is dark and has vicious spikes.

OPPOSITE—Small steps lead onto the garden path which, because of the dense planting, is nearly inaccessible. Having to push through vegetation enhances the feeling of being in a jungle. Tall plants on the left-hand side of the path screen the garden wall and what lies beyond. At the end of the path, on the left, a *Catalpa x erubescens* 'Purpurea' towers above all other planting.

ABOVE—A view from the end of the garden shows a different range of plants with finer leaves. As they are along the path they can be observed up close and don't need the boldness of leaves which must be viewed from further away.

TROPICAL PARADISE

In the centre of Norwich, surrounded by concrete, the most beautiful tropical paradise took root over several decades beginning in 1982 and created by the late Will Giles. On entering the garden through a forest of bamboo, the modern world seemed thousands of miles away.

This tropical paradise was one of the first examples of the exotic-style garden outside of large botanical gardens. Inspired by travels to the Amazon and Indian jungles, Will Giles planted flamboyant, lush and brightly coloured plants, forever pushing the limits of what were supposedly non-hardy plants. He was a true pioneer in creating jungle gardens and although the garden no longer exists, his legacy lives on.

Throughout the garden narrow paths led from one interesting area to another, often densely planted to create a true sense of jungle exploration. Despite being on a south-facing slope, the upper canopy in the garden made it quite shady, ensuring large-leaved, shade-loving plants flourished along the paths. They also provided protection for more tender plants underneath. The narrow paths would lead to clearings and these often contained seating where you could rest awhile engulfed by the jungle plants around you.

Another benefit of having the small, winding paths through the garden was that you had a chance to get lost. Winding around, backing up on yourself and not being able to see any other paths made the garden more adventurous as well as making it seem bigger than it was. To lose your sense of direction and get lost is probably the best compliment for the layout of the paths in a jungle garden.

Form and texture were very important in Will Giles's garden. Plants with strong shapes and textures were used as a basis for the garden, which was supplemented by adding annuals or other more tender plants. Creating a framework with hardy, evergreen plants such as *Aucuba japonica* 'Crotonifolia', *Phyllostachys nigra* and *Cordyline* means even in winter there will be good interest in the garden.

OPPOSITE—An open space outside a building within the garden has a sunny aspect. The succulents and other sun-loving, drought-tolerant plants located here cope with the full sun and dry soil.

ABOVE—Narrow paths surrounded by dense planting give a true feeling of jungle exploration.

An unusual structure in the garden was the tree house. This elevated garden room was a perfect place to relax and look down on the garden. It showed the array of large-leaved plants such as *Dicksonia antarctica* and *Tetrapanax* which were used, but also gave a good display of all the upper-canopy plants which were so important for the garden. From up there you could spend ages being absorbed by all the different shapes and sizes of all the foliage plants.

Other buildings within the garden were planted with climbers which had lush foliage. It seemed as if the jungle could absorb them at any moment, which is a credit to the plantsmanship of the owner; he made any maintenance and pruning back seem natural and organic. Around the veranda of the building, dense planting with lush foliage plants such as *Ensete ventricosum* 'Maurelii' meant that any view to the outside was partially obscured, enticing people to go out and explore what was beyond their immediate vision.

ABOVE—The tree house offers a perfect place to relax and get a bird's-eye view of the garden.

OPPOSITE TOP—Small buildings in the garden, overgrown with lush foliage, making them seem as if at any point the jungle could absorb them.

OPPOSITE BOTTOM A pot display of succulents on either side of the steps gives an immediate feeling of being surrounded by plants.

THE JUNGLE GARDEN

CHAPTER 5

Cultivating
Jungle Plants

The cultivation of jungle plants is not much different from that of other garden plants, for a jungle garden can be created using perennials, shrubs, trees and bulbs. Tender plants which may be included can be sown freshly each year or overwintered as cuttings or houseplants. To encourage plants to put on a lot of growth and create lush foliage, soil preparation and coppicing of trees are useful techniques – and there are many easy tricks for creating the jungle look that don't take up a lot of time.

Soil preparation

To achieve lush green or variegated foliage, it is important to start with good soil preparation by means of the addition of organic matter. This could be farmyard manure, but if your soil is quite rich already, or if your garden is on heavy clay, then you could consider adding coconut coir to it. Made from coconut husks, this product is a by-product of the coconut industry. You can buy it in small bags in garden centres, but if you want a larger amount you will find it in bulk at some nurseries. It is often recycled from strawberry or tomato growers as they usually get rid of this growing medium after a season.

An added bonus of using coconut coir is that you are not using peat, which comes from irreplaceable peat bogs that are environmentally important both as habitats and as carbon sinks, absorbing carbon dioxide from the atmosphere. Coconut coir is not just a good alternative for soil improvement, it is also ideal for potted plants. The coir is moisture-retentive and, unlike peat-based products, still absorbs water if it has dried out completely. The loose, grainy structure also means it drains freely and doesn't become too compacted for the roots to penetrate. Any growing medium for pot plants is only there to give the roots something to grow in; it doesn't need to have any nutrients itself as these can be added by using liquid fertilizer or slow-release fertilizer granules. Even plants that need ericaceous soil can grow in coconut coir, which in itself is pH neutral. To grow these plants you can simply feed them once a month with a liquid fertilizer which is made from seaweed with added sequestered iron, or slow-release granules for ericaceous plants can be added to the compost every six months.

Jungle plants generally produce a large amount of foliage in a relatively short amount of time, so they will do better when they get some extra fertilizer. Whether it is liquid or granulated, the fertilizer should contain a good amount of nitrogen as this is one of the components of chlorophyll.

TOP—Coconut coir is a peat-free soil improver or growing medium.

BOTTOM—Adding organic matter to your soil will improve the structure.

Plants use chlorophyll in combination with energy from sunlight to produce sugars from water and carbon dioxide, a process called photosynthesis. If a plant can't produce enough chlorophyll this process is not as efficient and the plant will not grow as well. So if the lush jungle look is what you are after, you need to make sure the plant is not lacking important nutrients.

Coppicing

There are some tricks to make plants produce larger leaves that don't involve fertilizing. Some plants, especially some trees and shrubs, respond very well to being cut back hard. Called coppicing, this technique is often used on sweet chestnut in productive woodland. If it is done regularly, the tree will start to compensate for the amount of branches and leaves it has lost by producing an abundance of branches that will shoot straight up and the leaves will grow larger because the plant is trying to capture as much sunlight as it can for growth. In the case of sweet chestnut this is done to produce straight stakes, but in a garden situation it will achieve plants with large leaves and straight stems. Plants such as *Catalpa*, *Liriodendron* and *Paulownia* are suited to this treatment.

Depending on the size of the plant when you put it in your garden, you can start coppicing it after one or two seasons. Cut the stems quite short, to about 30cm (12in) from the ground – though if the plant you want to coppice is behind taller plants, you could make the cut about 1m (3¼ft) from the ground, to turn it into more of a standard tree. Once your plant is established you can do this coppicing every year. I cut my *Catalpa* and *Paulownia* to about 30cm (12in) from the ground and they tend to shoot up at least 2–3m (6½–10ft) that same year. The leaves grow two or three times as big as on a tree which hasn't been coppiced. When the buds start growing in spring I tend to remove most of them so that the plants will put all their energy into the remaining buds, making for an even larger display.

As well as affecting the plant's size, coppicing enhances leaf colour. Especially with the purple-leaved *Catalpa*, the colours will be much darker than on trees which haven't been coppiced. *Liriodendron* (tulip tree) can also be coppiced, but even pollarding, where instead of cutting the entire plant down the the side branches are reduced heavily, will also give larger leaves with better colour. One *Liriodendron* to look out for is the species *L. chinense* which, when pollarded or coppiced, will produce large leaves that are deep purple when they emerge.

FROM LEFT TO RIGHT—The previous year's growth can be left on the plant until early spring. Especially in colder areas, cutting it down before winter can cause frost damage to the stems.

Make a cut just above a bud. Use clean, sharp tools for this to prevent unnecessary damage which can let diseases take hold.

All branches can be cut off to about 30cm (12in) above ground level. The plant will soon shoot up again and will have larger, more colourful foliage.

Cutting back

Herbaceous perennials are a good addition to any jungle garden. Their fast growth can quickly produce that look of denseness which is needed for the tropical effect and their hardiness means that you don't have to buy a new plant every year. Perennials come in a huge variety of leaf shapes and textures, from the large round leaf of *Petasites* to the linear leaf of the hardy sunflower *Helianthus* and all other shapes and sizes in between, meaning that they can truly achieve a perfect mix of visual interest.

Some evergreen herbaceous perennials, for example *Kniphofia*, don't need a lot of maintenance; you can just pull out the old leaves in spring and cut the flower stems down as low as you can in autumn. Other herbaceous perennials die back completely and the entire plant will need cutting down. Plants in this category will turn brown and brittle in autumn, but they are best not cut back straight away; the ideal time for this is early spring, as the stems or dead leaves give some protection to the crown of the plant throughout winter. The seed heads can also look attractive, as well as providing food and shelter for birds and invertebrates.

When cutting back your perennials, make sure you cut them down as low as you can. Leaving 10cm (4in) dead sticks doesn't give an attractive appearance and they can be a feeding ground for pests and diseases. Ideally, cut your plants to the ground completely, making sure not to cut into any green parts which are emerging from the ground.

FROM LEFT TO RIGHT—
The brown stems of hardy perennials are dead, but can be left throughout winter as they provide habitat for wildlife.

Cutting back hardy perennials in early spring ensures no new growth is damaged. The stems have all died, so need to be cut back as low as possible.

The plant has been cut right down to prevent congestion and stop diseases from establishing on the dead twigs.

Potting up

Pot displays can be very useful in jungle gardens, especially on hardstanding areas such as patios. The display can be changed as the seasons go by, as plants that may look good in spring can be put at the front during their peak time and moved further back once they have gone over. Using pots also means you can grow plants that may become a bit invasive in the garden. Although care against spreading still needs to be taken as plants can self-seed or their roots can grow through the hole in the bottom of the pot, it is less likely that plants such as variegated ground elder (*Aegopodium*), variegated Japanese knotweed *(Reynoutria)* or mare's tail *(Equisetum)* end up taking over your garden. Plants in pots tend to come up a bit earlier in spring, too, because the soil is well drained and thus warms up quicker. It is an easy way to extend the jungle season.

Plants can grow in the same pot for quite some time, provided they get a regular feed. If they do outgrow their pot and become root-bound, they will need to be potted on to a larger container, though on the whole it only needs to be about 10cm (4in) wider than the old one. Fast-spreading plants can be potted on more generously in terms of space. Some people place broken shards of terracotta pots or grit in the base of the pot to increase drainage, but in my experience it doesn't make any difference.

Place some coconut coir or another peat-free compost in the bottom of the pot, then position the plant in the middle of its new pot and gently scatter some compost around the edge. Once this rim has been filled with compost, press it down gently with the tips of your fingers, making sure not to compact it too much. Top up with compost and repeat until the new compost is level with the soil in which the plant is growing. The final step is to water the plant in to make sure any large air pockets are filled with the compost. It may need a bit more topping up, but if you have been thorough in pushing the compost around the rim this shouldn't be necessary.

FAR LEFT—The healthy root system of this *Astelia nervosa* 'Son of Red Devil' has filled the pot, so it needs repotting.

ABOVE LEFT—The pot is filled with peat-free compost, making sure there are no air gaps along the side by gently pushing the compost down.

ABOVE RIGHT—Once the compost has been topped up all around the edges the plant can be watered in.

Taking cuttings

Cuttings are an easy way to get more of your favourite plants for free. It is also a great way to overwinter more tender plants if you haven't got enough indoor space. Plants such as *Saccharum officinarum* var. *violaceum* (purple sugar cane) will root very easily in a jar of water, and are happy to be left in this until spring. Another plant which takes very well from cuttings is *Persicaria microcephala* 'Red Dragon'.

You can take cuttings whenever there is cutting material on the plant, even in late autumn or very early spring. To do this, you need to cut just under a leaf, making sure the cutting is 10–20cm (4–8in) long. Once the cut has been made, strip off the bottom leaves and cut the rest of the leaves in half; the plant won't have a root system to draw water from and if there is less leaf surface then evaporation will be less too, ensuring the plant doesn't wilt before it grows roots.

Once the cutting is prepared, place it in a jar of water, ensuring none of the leaves are beneath the surface. In the case of *Persicaria* roots will start to appear within a week, but with some other plants this can take several weeks. When the cuttings in the jar have a good root system, pot them up in 9cm (3½in) pots and plant them out once the roots start growing through the holes in the base of the pot.

FAR LEFT—When taking cuttings, choose healthy shoots.

ABOVE LEFT—Take the cutting just below a leaf. Before putting the cuttings in water, take off the bottom leaves and cut the top leaves in half to prevent too much evaporation.

ABOVE RIGHT—Once roots appear and start branching out, pot up the plants individually.

Pests

Pests and diseases can appear on any plant, and some of the more tender species can be affected by greenhouse pests as there is no cold period to push back their numbers. Good hygiene is always very important, meaning that weeds or plant remains are cleared regularly and the entire greenhouse gets a scrub down before any plants are placed in it in autumn. Washing up liquid and water can be used for this cleaning.

Predators and pesticides

When growing plants in a greenhouse or any other enclosed environment the use of natural predators can be very effective. These predators can be ordered online and often come on cards or in little sachets which can be hung on plants. The predators will eat the adult pests or their eggs and larvae and can even be put in preventively in some cases. If you wish to use a pesticide, it is important to only buy a biological one which isn't residual; any chemical, non-selective pest control will also kill the pests' natural predators, even weeks after it has been applied. If you bring in the natural predators yourself, do not apply any pesticides at all.

Greenfly, aphids and caterpillars

Greenfly and aphids can appear throughout the year, but will often manifest themselves on plants kept in the greenhouse over winter and natural predators can be used here. If the plants are outside, these pests can be controlled by spraying with a fatty acid-based pesticide or a plant invigorator – the latter contains seaweed extract which will also provide a foliar feed to the plant, making it more resilient against pests and diseases. A sprayer filled with a few drops of washing up liquid topped up with water can also be effective. The soap, or fatty acid, will dissolve the protective layer of the pests, after which they will dry out. This also works on caterpillars, the presence of which can be recognized by large holes in the centre and around the edges of leaves.

If there is an attack of soft scale, it is important to spray the entire plant, including the bottom of the leaves as often they hide there. Soft scale can be spotted quite easily as the leaves of a plant will have a grey, mouldy layer. This mould lives on the secretions of soft scale and once the pest has been treated, the staining should disappear also.

Slugs

Slugs munch their way especially quickly through thinner-leaved foliage plants. The damage is recognized by slug trails and holes around the edges of the leaves; often the leaf looks shredded, with only the veins left and all the soft tissue between them eaten away. If you have a lot of slugs in your garden, a regular soil treatment with nematodes can work very well. The nematodes eat the slugs and will even attack the smallest ones, which are often not affected by slug pellets. A similar nematode treatment can also be given to plants which suffer from vine weevil. Often prevalent in container plants, the grubs eat all the roots, which make the plant look as if it needs water.

LEFT—Slug damage on a pelargonium.

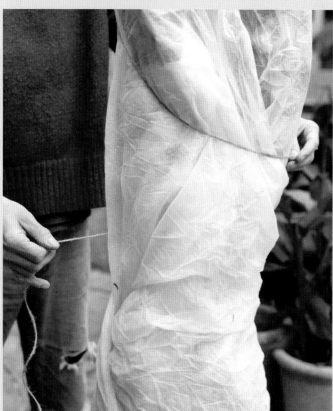

THE JUNGLE GARDEN

Overwintering

Some plants need protection in winter and as tempting as it might be on sunny February days, they shouldn't be placed outside until night temperatures are at least 10°C (50°F), which tends to be in late spring. If plants are taken out too early a cold spell will cause brown patches on the leaves and they may drop off, or develop a purple sheen. Some will recover, but for plants that have soft, non-woody stems even one cold night can be fatal.

A plant which may need winter protection is *Musa basjoo*, the Japanese banana, which can often be found in plant nurseries. The large, paddle-shaped leaves give the garden a tropical jungle look. Protecting this plant over winter means it will achieve its full potential. As a herbaceous perennial the *Musa basjoo* will die down to the ground in cold winters. The plant will overwinter on underground parts and will shoot up again in spring. If we want to grow or retain taller stems then they can be protected by wrapping them up with garden fleece or hessian. In very cold areas an extra layer of straw can be added around the stems before the plant is wrapped up. By doing this the height of the stems is retained which means the plant will form part of the upper canopy within the jungle garden. The same method can be applied to other slightly tender plants such as *Musella lasiocarpa* or *Tetrapanax papyrifer* 'Rex'.

OPPOSITE—*Musella lasiocarpa* can stay outside in colder areas when it is protected. Side leaves are cut back so the fleece fits around the plant snuggly. String is tied around the wrapped up plant to ensure the fleece stays in place during winter.

ABOVE—This *Schefflera* was taken outside too early and a late frost caused the brown discoloration of the leaf.

Growing and thinning out bamboo

Bamboo is perfect for any jungle garden as it reaches its full height in one growing season, so it can quickly form a screen or provide dappled shade for other plants near it. Some people are very hesitant about growing it because of its invasiveness, but there are some species, such as *Himalayacalamus falconeri*, which will not spread but slowly form a clump. Others that are more invasive can easily be grown in pots or raised beds. Bamboos don't like drying out when they are pot-grown, so *Phyllostachys*, for instance, is best grown in a pot that is either sitting in a saucer or in a tub without holes and in a location which isn't too exposed to the prevailing wind. However, if a bamboo does dry out it will usually recover. Black bamboo, *Phyllostachys nigra*, is not suitable for growing in pots, since it will go brown if it dries out even slightly.

The crown of bamboo can be lifted to show off the stems even more. In spring, cut the thinnest shoots down to the ground, leaving only the thicker, well-developed stems. Once you have done this, remove the side shoots up to 1m (3¼ft) from the ground. This can be done on all stems or, to make it look more natural, on half of them.

LEFT—To create a nicer display, the smallest bamboo shoots can be cut right down to the ground.

RIGHT—Taking off the side shoots up to 1m (3¼ft) ensures the beautiful yellow stems of *Phyllostachys aurea* are shown off.

Weeding

The advantage of jungle gardens is that the denser the vegetation, the more the resemblance to a real jungle, and an undergrowth of certain plants gives a pleasing effect. Fortunately, weeding doesn't tend to be a lot of work in a garden where foliage covers most of the ground as conditions are often too dark and dense for any weeds to grow underneath. Most weeding will have to be done in late spring or early summer as at that point the canopy may not have completely covered the soil underneath and plants won't be as densely packed as later in the year. Make sure the roots of the weeds come out of the ground completely and that you remove them before they are in flower – some plants, such as thistles, will push their last energy into producing seeds so if you take them in flower and leave them somewhere on a pile in the garden, it is very likely they will still produce seed. The roots of any pernicious weeds need to be dug out as much as possible and should not be put on a compost heap. With these particular weeds it is worth daily checks, removing any greenery that comes up. Eventually the plant will not have enough reserve energy to produce further growth.

ABOVE—When weeding out plants with tap roots it is important to make sure the entire root is dug up.

CHAPTER 6

A–Z of Jungle Plants

There is a very large range of plants suitable for the jungle garden. Many are easy to obtain while others will need to be bought from specialist nurseries. Hunting down the plants is part of the thrill of creating a jungle garden and getting hold of rarer plants means your visitors will be excited and curious to see what hidden gems lie around the corner. Having said that, it is very much possible to create a stunning jungle garden with plants from the local garden centre. This A-Z represents my 'desert island plants' and I hope it will help you seek out your perfect jungle plants.

A

Acanthus sennii

Ethiopian acanthus

Origin:	Minimum
Ethiopia	temperature:
	-5°C (23°F)
Position:	Maximum height:
Full sun	*1.5m (5ft)*

Every plant directory has to start with
an *Acanthus*. Apart from the familiar
A. mollis with its beautiful leaves, the
more unusual *A. sennii* is well worth
growing. The leaves are very spiky
and look like holly. It loves a sunny,
dry location and in colder areas will
die back, but if it doesn't get too wet
in winter it usually shoots up again
from the base and can grow 60–70cm
(2–2¼ft) in a year.

Acer palmatum

Japanese maple

Origin:	Minimum
Japan	temperature:
	-20°C (-4°F)
Position:	Maximum height:
Partial shade	*3m (10ft)*

There are many cultivars of *Acer
palmatum* and all have their own
appeal. This small tree has palmate
foliage but some cultivar leaves are
thin as threads, so will appear very
linear or even filigree. Acer *palmatum*
'Koto-ito-komachi' and 'Red Pygmy'
are two such cultivars, while Acer
palmatum 'Baldsmith' has leaves
that look like intricate lace. The
colour range of Japanese maples is
extensive. Acer *palmatum* 'Ukigomo'
(opposite) emerges with pink leaves
in spring and then turns to almost
pure white during most of summer.
Later in the year the leaves will colour
up to mottled green. Because of the
extremely low amount of chlorophyl
in the leaf this cultivar is very slow
growing. All Japanese maples have
amazing autumn colours ranging
from bright yellow to vibrant red.

Adiantum venustum

Maidenhair fern

Origin:	Minimum
China	temperature:
	-20°C (-4°F)
Position:	Maximum height:
Partial to full shade	*20cm (8in)*

Adiantum venustum is often sold as a
houseplant but can thrive outdoors
too. If it is planted in the right
position it will gradually spread
through the border, where the soft,
filigree foliage weaves bolder leaf
structures together. As a houseplant
it can be quite fussy as it will shrivel
up the moment it doesn't have enough
water. When it is planted outside,
make sure the area doesn't dry out.

Aegopodium podograria

Ground elder

Origin: *Europe/Asia*	Minimum temperature: *-20°C (-4°F)*
Position: *Partial to full shade*	Maximum height: *25cm (10in)*

Many gardeners will have come across ground elder at some point. This often pernicious weed is not something that should be planted in the garden, but there are a few cultivars that can brighten up a patio area if they are kept in a pot. 'Variegatum', 'Dangerous' (above) and 'Gold Marbled' are all forms with white or yellow variegation. One very well-behaved cultivar is 'Bengt', which has inward-curling leaves and is the slowest grower of them all. The lanceolate leaflets can give a great texture to a pot display and the white flowers will be loved by pollinators. Make sure to remove the seedheads before they spread.

Aeonium 'Zwartkop'

Tree houseleek

Origin: *South Africa*	Minimum temperature: *5°C (41°F)*
Position: *Full sun*	Maximum height: *1m (3¼ft)*

This succulent does very well in dry gardens. The cultivar 'Zwartkop' has dark leaves which will become almost black when it is in full sun. They can be grown in pots very well but will need a well-draining sandy compost mixture as the roots will rot if they become too wet. It is not hardy, so will need to be overwintered in a frost-free place where it is kept dry. *Aeonium* is easily grown from cuttings by pushing stems into a mix of sand and compost.

Agave montana

Agave

Origin: *Mexico*	Minimum temperature: *-10°C (14°F)*
Position: *Full sun*	Maximum height: *1m (3¼ft)*

Agave can be very spiky, and *A. montana* from the mountainous parts of Mexico scores a ten out of ten on the spikiness scale. Not only does it have huge spikes at the tips of the linear leaves, it also has rose-like thorns all along the leaf edge. A very hardy succulent which loves a sunny and dry position, in a pot it can be a real focal point – just make sure you never have to move it, or even walk close to it, as you will be caught by the spikes.

Amicia zygomeris

Amicia

Origin:	Minimum
Mexico	temperature:
	-10°C (14°F)
Position:	Maximum height:
Full sun to	*1.5m (5ft)*
partial shade	

A herbaceous perennial in regions where the temperature doesn't drop below -10°C (14°F), *Amicia* can easily be overwintered in cooler areas by taking cuttings in autumn. The plant is part of the pea family, which becomes evident when the yellow flowers appear as they resemble those of sweet pea. The main attraction of the plant is the leaves, which have an elongated heart shape and in the evening start to droop, as if the plant goes to sleep for the night. It prefers moisture-retentive soil but can also be grown in drier spots where it won't be quite as tall.

Aloiampelos striatula

Hardy aloe

Origin:	Minimum
South Africa	temperature:
	-15°C (5°F)
Position:	Maximum height:
Full sun to	*1m (3¼ft)*
partial shade	

This hardy succulent is great in a pot or open ground in a sunny, dry spot. Despite its succulent and spiky appearance, its hardiness has been proved through winters with icy temperatures and snow inflicting hardly any damage on the plant. In summer, orange-yellow flower spikes form an attractive feature above the fleshy and slightly spiky linear leaves. It is fast growing in the right spot.

Aralia bipinnata

Devil's walking stick

Origin:	Minimum
Taiwan, China	temperature:
	-20°C (-4°F)
Position:	Maximum height:
Full sun to	*4m (12ft)*
dappled shade	

'Devil's walking stick' derived its name from the amount of spikes it has on the stems and leaves. The little lanceolate leaflets which form the leaf are dark green and turn a beautiful red and yellow in autumn. When the shrub matures it is ideal as an upper canopy plant where it will provide shade and shelter to undergrowth, as well as filtering the light beautifully.

Arthropodium candidum 'Little Lilia'

Dwarf rock lily

Origin:	Minimum
New Zealand	temperature:
	0°C (32°F)
Position:	Maximum height:
Dappled shade	*25cm (10in)*

This plant has linear cream and green variegated leaves and long upright stems of small white flowers that bloom in summer, giving it a nice airiness. In a very sheltered garden it could be left outside in winter, but it's better to bring it indoors. It is an ideal plant to grow in a pot in a shadier spot, where it will brighten up the garden.

Aspidistra elatior

Cast iron plant

Origin:	Minmum
Japan	temperature:
	-20°C (-4°F)
Position:	Maximum height:
Dappled shade	*90cm (3ft)*
to full shade	

Mostly sold as a green houseplant, this aspidistra thrives on neglect. Not many people realize how hardy it is until they move it outdoors and find that several winters later it is still alive. However, aspidistras don't like having wet feet, so grow it in well-drained soil or in a large pot. The upright, linear leaves are evergreen and can be completely green or variegated as in *Aspidistra elatior* 'Variegata' (above). Slugs may damage the leaves, which can be prevented by applying nematodes. Another very hardy species to look out for is *Aspidistra sichuanensis*, which usually has spotted leaves.

Asplenium scolopendrium

Hart's tongue fern

Origin:	Minimum
Europe	temperature:
	-25°C (-13°F)
Position:	Maximum height:
Partial shade	*50cm (1½ft)*
to full shade	

This fern with linear foliage is often seen growing out of ancient walls. It loves high humidity, but even soils which are on the drier side can be suitable for it. The evergreen foliage doesn't need cutting back until early spring. Later in spring the new fronds will unfurl beautifully, which is always a feast for the eye. The cultivar pictured above, *Asplenium scolopendrium* 'Golden Queen' (Crispum Group), has a wavy leaf edge and a golden colour which will become bright yellow in a site with some sunshine. This fern is very easy to grow but can take a couple of years to establish.

Astilboides
tabularis

Common astilboides

Origin:	Minimum
China	temperature:
	-20°C (-4°F)
Position:	Maximum height:
Full shade	80cm (2½ft)

This is one of those plants which deserves to be grown more. The beautiful, dinner-plate-sized leaves have a Jurassic texture, like you would imagine dinosaur skin to be, and a bright green colour. They form a great combination with finer leaves such as grasses or ferns. *Astilboides* prefers deep shade and quite wet soil as on drier soils the leaves will turn brown rapidly. Its hardiness makes it one of the best herbaceous perennials for the damper jungle garden.

Athyrium
filix-femina
'Dre's Dagger'

Lady fern

Origin:	Minimum
Japan	temperature:
	-20°C (-4°F)
Position:	Maximum height:
Shade	70cm (2¼ft)

'Dre's Dagger' is a lady fern cultivar which has very different filigree foliage to other members of *Athyrium*; the individual leaflets on the fronds are at an angle which makes it look as if they are zig-zagging. Each of the leaflets has a tiny crest at the end, which adds to the overall texture of the plant. It is a very unusual cultivar which can be bought at specialist nurseries. 'Victoriae' is similar, so would be a good alternative.

Astelia chathamica

Maori flax

Origin:	Minimum
New Zealand	temperature:
	-5°C (23°F)
Position:	Maximum height:
Full sun to	1.2m (4ft)
partial shade	

Astelia chathamica has linear foliage which can be silver-grey or red. Mature plants have a beautiful upright habit and can be grown in full sun. It is evergreen and will add good structure to the garden any time of the year.

B

Azara microphylla 'Variegata'

Chocolate bush

Origin:
South America

Minimum temperature:
-15°C (5°F)

Position:
Full sun to full shade

Maximum height:
3m (10ft)

The minute, round leaves of this evergreen shrub are a good combination with large, bold leaves. It is a great boundary plant and the variegated form will light up darker corners. Make sure to plant it in a sheltered spot, since winds early in the year can scorch the young growth. Apart from its attractive foliage, it produces tiny yellow flowers in winter which can fill the entire garden with the scent of chocolate and vanilla. If grown in a pot it can be kept small by pinching out the new growth in spring.

Athyrium niponicum var. pictum 'Ursula's Red'

Painted fern

Origin:
Japan

Minimum temperature:
-25°C (-13°F)

Position:
Dappled shade to full shade

Maximum height:
30cm (12in)

The painted ferns are the most colourful of ferns; their foliage may be silver or have bands of dark red and purple. The filigree shape and colour of the leaves makes them an excellent companion to larger leaves such as those of hostas. They don't like to dry out completely as they will soon scorch and turn brown.

Begonia 'Benitochiba'

Begonia

Origin:
Japan

Minimum temperature:
-5°C (23°F)

Position:
Dappled shade

Maximum height:
30cm (12in)

Begonia 'Benitochiba' (opposite) has palmate leaves with lance-shaped leaflets. The young growth is pink but will turn into a silver leaf with dark purple veins. It is one of the hardier begonias as it can take a few degrees of frost if it is grown in a well-drained soil or in a pot.

Begonia koelzii

Begonia

Origin:	Minimum
India	temperature:
	-5°C (23°F)
Position:	Maximum height:
Shade	50cm (20in)

Originally found by botanist and plant hunter Francis Kingdon-Ward in Manipur, this *Begonia* species seems hardy. It will die back in winter, but by the end of spring the leaves will be up to 50cm (20in) tall again. The spotted leaf stalks with very pointy, palmate leaves give extra colour to the plant. For extra winter protection the plant can be mulched with compost or leaf mould in autumn.

Begonia luxurians

Palm-leaf begonia

Origin:	Minimum
Brazil	temperature:
	5°C (41°F)
Position:	Maximum height:
Dappled shade	2m (6½ft)

Within the genus *Begonia* there are some stunning foliage plants that will enrich any jungle garden and *B. luxurians* is one of these, looking rather like a small palm tree. The palmate leaf has individual lobes that resemble long fingers. This plant doesn't like full sunshine and certainly doesn't want to dry out. A monthly feed of seaweed extract will ensure good growth with healthy, green leaves. *B. luxurians* isn't hardy but easy to overwinter by cutting back the stems and placing in a frost-free garage or somewhere else indoors.

Begonia variegata

Begonia

Origin:	Minimum
China	temperature:
	5°C (41°F)
Position:	Maximum height:
Dappled shade to full shade	25cm (10in)

Begonia variegata has light green leaves with distinctive brown markings and a brown edging all round that frames the colours of the leaf very neatly. When this plant is grown in shade the leaves will grow larger than when it is grown in more light. It prefers a well-drained position and is best grown in a pot so it can be put indoors before the first frost and grown as a very attractive houseplant in winter.

Boehmeria platanifolia

False nettle

Origin:	Minimum temperature:
Japan	-20°C (-4°F)
Position:	Maximum height:
Dappled shade	*1m (3¼ft)*

Boehmeria platanifolia is part of the nettle family and a recent introduction at specialist nurseries. The leaves are round with a point at the end, making them look like little stingrays. It is originally a woodland plant, so it prefers dappled shade in moisture-retentive soil. *Boehmeria* forms a small-sized shrub so can be planted further to the back of the border, or form a screen on the corner of a path. The distinct leaf shape combines well with linear and filigree foliage. Other Japanese woodland plants such as *Hakonechloa macra* or *Athyrium niponicum* var. *pictum* 'Ursula's Red' form a good combination with this *Boehmeria*.

Borinda papyrifera CS1046

Blue dragon bamboo

Origin:	Minimum temperature:
China	-15°C (5°F)
Position:	Maximum height:
Full sun to dappled shade	*4m (13ft)*

This hardy, clump-forming bamboo will not take over your entire garden. This form with only a collection number was collected by Christopher Stapleton in Yunnan, China, and has an extraordinary blue-grey stem colour. This colour is most pronounced early in the season on the young stems, especially when the plant is grown in drier soils. The rustling of the leaves gives a calming effect and will mute noises from beyond the garden. A good plant to be in a prominent position or as a boundary plant.

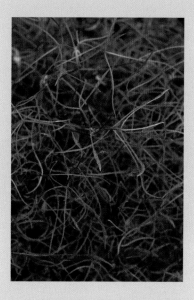

Broussonetia papyrifera 'Laciniata'

Paper mulberry

Origin:	Minimum temperature:
China	-15°C (5°F)
Position:	Maximum height:
Full sun	*1m (3¼ft)*

The dark filigree foliage of this small shrub combines perfectly with larger leaves. It stays quite small and is slow growing, so can be placed at the front of a border, or in a pot. Sometimes thin, thread-like leaves can burn in a sunny and dry position, but with *Broussonetia papyrifera* 'Laciniata' this is not the case. Even in full sun it will look attractive and have a good, dark colour.

Brassaiopsis mitis

Brassaiopsis

Origin: Taiwan, China	Minimum temperature: -10°C (14°F)
Position: Partial shade	Maximum height: 3–5m (10–16ft) after 10 years

Brassaiopsis mitis is the ultimate foliage plant for any leaf-shape enthusiast. The palmate leaves are attached in the centre then spread out and form an oval ending. The stems form another attraction as they have thick thorns all along them. Although it seems very tropical it grows in the same region as *Tetrapanax* and is therefore as hardy as those plants. It can be grown in a pot as well as in the border and prefers partial/dappled shade in the morning as afternoon sun can be too hot and scorch the leaves. It prefers moisture-retentive soil and does not like drying out. Aphids can sometimes damage the new growth, so regular inspection and a spray with an organic plant invigorator is advisable to prevent this from happening. This plant is only available in specialist nurseries and won't be cheap to buy. However, the shape of the leaf is so unusual it is really worth obtaining one.

Canna

Canna lily

Origin: South Africa	Minimum temperature: -10°C (14°F)
Position: Full sun to partial shade	Maximum height: 1.5m (5ft)

With their large leaves and often bright flowers, cannas give a tropical jungle look to any garden. They prefer moisture-retentive soil in full sun to partial shade and are surprisingly hardy on well-drained soils. Leave the stems and leaves until after the first frost has turned them brown, then cut them to ground level and place the leaves and stems over the crown for a bit of extra protection. *Canna* 'Durban' (opposite) has dark leaves with bright red and yellow stripes all along the leaf and orange flowers; its sister 'Pretoria' has green leaves with yellow stripes and yellow flowers. *Canna* 'Musifolia' is grown for its green foliage with a reddish tint, as it will only flower in long, hot summers. In colder areas the rhizomes of *Canna* can be lifted in late autumn and stored dry in a crate.

Capsicum annuum 'Calico'

Chilli

Origin: South America	Minimum temperature: 5°C (41°F)
Position: Sunny	Maximum height: 30cm (12in)

Chillies aren't often used as a foliage plant, but the cultivar 'Calico' with variegated purple and white leaves is a colourful addition to the jungle garden. It produces fragrant purple chillies and can be grown from seed every spring. This plant requires a well-drained position and in full sunshine the colours of the leaves will be more vibrant.

Catalpa

Indian bean tree

Origin: *China*	Minimum temperature: *-20°C (-4°F)*
Position: *Partial shade to full sun*	Maximum height: *2.5m (8½ft) if coppiced annually*

Indian bean trees are known for their large leaves and respond well to coppicing. If this is done in late winter or early spring the new leaves will be larger and have a more intense colour than when the plant is left unpruned. Another benefit of annual coppicing is that the tree will respond by putting on a lot of growth, often producing shoots 2.5m (8½ft) tall that same year. Although a large tree, by pruning it back every year it can easily be grown in small and medium-sized gardens. *Catalpa* x *erubescens* 'Purpurea' produces nearly black leaves after annual coppicing and *C. bignonioides* 'Aurea' (above) is a golden form.

Carica x pentagona (syn. Vasconcellea x heilbornii)

Babaco

Origin: *Ecuador*	Minimum temperature: *5°C (41°F)*
Position: *Full sun to dappled shade*	Maximum height: *2m (6½ft)*

This relative of papaya is found at high altitudes and this means it is more cold-tolerant than papaya itself. It bears only female flowers, which could produce fruit in warmer areas. The pointy leaf is large and has pink veins, giving it a subtle difference to any green leaves around it. It will need to be taken under cover in autumn and can be grown in pots.

Castanea sativa 'Variegata'

Variegated sweet chestnut

Origin: *Southern Europe*	Minimum temperature: *-25°C (-13°F)*
Position: *Full sun to dappled shade*	Maximum height: *2m (6½ft) if coppiced annually*

Sweet chestnuts are beautiful trees with serrated, lance-shaped leaves. On this variegated form (opposite) the white edges give them a real freshness and sparkle. Chestnuts are often coppiced for producing fence posts and this one is just as happy to be cut down as its green parent. However, the leaves will have a brighter white and will be larger than when it is not cut back.

Clivia miniata

Clivia

Origin:	Minimum temperature:
South Africa	5°C (41°F)
Position:	Maximum height:
Dappled shade to full shade	60cm (2ft)

The round-ended, linear leaves of *Clivia* are a good combination with filigree ferns or lance-shaped foliage. Used as a houseplant since Victorian times, both the green and variegated forms such as 'Striata' (above) or the banded type 'Akebono' will brighten up dark corners. In very sheltered areas with a minimum amount of frost they can survive outdoors all year. *Clivia* can produce green, yellow and orange flowers in winter.

Colocasia

Elephant's ear

Origin:	Minimum temperature:
Asia	-10°C (14°F)
Position:	Maximum height:
Partial shade, sheltered	80cm (2½ft)

There are many different *Colocasia* for sale and a lot of them are very difficult to overwinter, but *Colocasia esculenta* 'Pink China' (above) is very reliable and hardy. This cultivar has been known to survive quite harsh winters with snow and ice outside in a pot. They don't like to dry out and they will appreciate a soil with plenty of organic matter and a weekly feed of liquid seaweed. *Colocasia gaoligongensis* is hardy to -10°C (14°F) which will grow to 1.2m (4ft) tall.

Convallaria majalis 'Albostriata'

Variegated lily-of-the-valley

Origin:	Minimum temperature:
Europe	-20°C (-4°F)
Position:	Maximum height:
Dappled shade to full shade	25cm (10in)

Lily-of-the-valley is a good groundcover for shady spots. The cultivar 'Albostriata' is one of many variegated forms which will brighten up dark corners with stripes of bright yellow along the leaves. If the plants are exposed to a lot of sunshine the leaves will scorch and often the plant will then become dormant early in the season. *Convallaria* prefers a soil rich in organic matter, so a winter mulch of leaf mould will ensure the plants perform at their best. Highly scented flowers will appear in spring.

Coronilla valentina subsp. glauca

Scorpion vetch

Origin:	Minimum
Southern Europe	temperature:
	-15°C (5°F)
Position:	Maximum height:
Full sun	*2m (6½ft)*

This scrambling shrub has delicate feathered leaves. The leaves can have a blue-grey hue or be variegated as in 'Variegata' (above). The cultivar 'Citrina' has lemon-yellow flowers which are lighter in colour than the other cultivars. The main flush of scented flowers appears in winter, but it will bear flowers for most of the year. *Coronilla* prefers full sunshine on a well-drained soil and can be grown against a wall or amongst large-leaved shrubs where it will soon weave through.

Cryptomeria japonica 'Rasen'

Twisted Japanese cedar

Origin:	Minimum
Japan	temperature:
	-20°C (-4°F)
Position:	Maximum height:
Full sun to	*4m (13ft)*
dappled shade	

The needles of this conifer twist around the branches, giving it a very unusual texture. It is a very upright plant so it won't take up too much space and will form a good, yet thin, upper canopy. This means that plants which prefer a bit more light will not be shaded out by this conifer. *Cryptomeria* don't mind drier sites in full sun and are fully hardy.

Cussonia paniculata

Spiked cabbage tree

Origin:	Minimum
South Africa	temperature:
	-5°C (23°F)
Position:	Maximum height:
Full sun	*2m (6½ft)*

The blue-grey palmate foliage of this plant is extraordinary in its shape as it looks like a large ice crystal. It is best to grow it in a pot as it doesn't like to be dug up for winter storage every year. However, in a sheltered and sunny spot this plant can stay outdoors all year and will grow to a good size.

Cyperus papyrus

Papyrus

Origin:	Minimum
Africa	temperature:
	10°C (50°F)
Position:	Maximum height:
Full sun	1.5m (5ft)

Papyrus was used to make parchment in ancient Egypt and was found in abundance throughout the Nile delta. It is a very attractive plant with tall green stems topped off by round heads, resembling an *Allium* seedhead. It doesn't take up much space and will easily weave its stems through other plants. Papyrus doesn't like drying out, so is ideally grown in a bucket or mini pond. In winter it needs to be taken indoors, but is very attractive as a houseplant.

Cyrtomium fortunei

Fortune's cyrtomium

Origin:	Minimum
Japan	temperature:
	-25°C (-13°F)
Position:	Maximum height:
Shade	40cm (16in)

This fern has sturdy, lance-shaped leaflets. The leaves are evergreen but in late winter they can be cut back to allow space for the new growth. Be very careful as new growth can develop quite early in the season. It forms a good combination with linear leaves such as those of *Hakonechloa macra*. This fern can be grown in a pot as well as in the border where it will soon fill out.

Dahlia imperialis

Tree dahlia

Origin:	Minimum
Central America	temperature:
	0°C (32°F)
Position:	Maximum height:
Dappled shade	3m (10ft)

The word 'dahlia' tends to conjure up colourful, big flowers, but many also have beautiful foliage. *Dahlia imperialis* is one of those that should be grown for its leaves rather than its blooms. The plant shoots up in spring and will soon reach a good height with lovely foliage. Only in very long summers might it get some flowers in mid to late autumn. One cultivar called 'Dia de los Muertos' produces nearly black new foliage.

Dahlia 'Woodbridge'

Dahlia

Origin:	**Minimum**
Central America	**temperature:**
	0°C (32°F)
Position:	**Maximum height:**
Full sun to	*75cm (2½ft)*
dappled shade	

During the *Dahlia* trials at RHS Wisley this cultivar was awarded an Award of Garden Merit for its foliage. It is indeed stunning with filigree foliage which combines very well with large, round leaves, so truly deserved this recognition. The plant itself needs a bit of support which can easily be achieved by planting it amongst sturdier plants and letting it scramble through. It is one of the last *Dahlia* to shoot up in spring so is best taken indoors for winter, kept dry, and then potted up in a greenhouse in March to give it a bit of a head start.

Dasylirion serratifolium

Sandpaper sotol

Origin:	**Minimum**
Mexico	**temperature:**
	-15°C (5°F)
Position:	**Maximum height:**
Full sun	*1m (3¼ft)*

This linear and upright plant is not one to put right next to a path as it has tiny needles all along its leaves. It is beautiful, though, and will do very well in the sunny and dry jungle garden where it will combine well with wider leaved plants such as *Agave* and *Opuntia*. It can sometimes produce a flower spike which can grow to 4m (13ft).

Dicksonia antarctica

Tree fern

Origin:	**Minimum**
Australia/Tasmania	**temperature:**
	-5°C (23°F)
Position:	**Maximum height:**
Dappled shade	*2.5m (8¼ft)*

Large tree ferns tend to be sold as loose trunks without any roots. Water both the crown as well as the base of the trunk – it is a common myth that only the top needs to be watered as supposedly the rest of the trunk is dead. When it is watered at the base a good root system will soon develop. It is an ideal plant to use as an upper canopy and one or more of these tree ferns planted in a garden give an instant jungle look. In colder areas the crown can be protected by placing straw in the centre and covering it in fleece. The fronds will unfurl beautifully in spring and can become 2m (6½ft) long.

E

Disporum longistylum 'Night Heron'

Fairy bells

Origin:	Minimum
China	temperature:
	-30°C (-22°F)
Position:	Maximum height:
Dappled shade	80cm (2½ft)
to full shade	

Disporum is a perennial plant which loves a humus-rich soil. It can tolerate deep shade, although some light will bring out the dark colour in 'Night Heron' a bit better. In spring this cultivar will come up almost black, but during the summer season it will gradually turn greener. The small, lance-shaped leaves don't suffer from pests or diseases.

Echeveria derenbergii

Mexican snow ball

Origin:	Minimum
Central America	temperature:
	1°C (34°F)
Position:	Maximum height:
Full sun	15cm (6in)

This pretty succulent has grey foliage which has a cushiony effect. They can be used as individual plants, but carpet planting is also very effective. *Echeveria* can tolerate full sunshine in dry conditions so is ideal for the sunny garden, or along a dry, south-facing wall. Small plantlets will form around the rosette; these can be broken off and potted up for overwintering on a sunny windowsill.

Elegia tectorum

Cape thatching reed

Origin:	Minimum
South Africa	temperature:
	-20°C (-4°F)
Position:	Maximum height:
Dappled shade	1m (3¼ft)

This member of the restio family has very sturdy shoots which are green with dark brown sheaths. They form a perfect dome and don't require a lot of maintenance. Any shoots which die back can easily be pulled out or cut down to ground level. It is a great plant to add an authentic Jurassic look to a jungle garden as restios were around some 60 million years ago. They can be planted near the edge of a border to show off their beautiful structure and combine well with plants with big leaves such as *Astilboides tabularis*.

Ensete ventricosum 'Maurelii'

Abyssinian banana

Origin:	Minimum temperature:
Eastern Africa	5°C (41°F)
Position:	Maximum height:
Full sun or dappled shade	3m (10ft)

Ensete ventricosum 'Maurelii' is part of the banana family and has very large, red, paddle-shaped leaves. This plant can reach a good height in one season, even if the base is quite small at the beginning of the year. *Ensete* can be difficult to overwinter, but a heated greenhouse would be perfect. Alternatively, they can be grown as a specimen houseplant during the cold season. If they are overwintered in a cold garage or loft, make sure to drain all the water out of them before storing. This can be done by cutting all the leaves off and placing the plant upside down for a few days. If they are too damp during winter they will quickly start rotting.

Equisetum 'Bandit'

Scouring rush

Origin:	Minimum temperature:
Japan	-20°C (-4°F)
Position:	Maximum height:
Dappled shade	40cm (16in)

Rushes are some of the oldest plants in existence and have been around for 100 million years. *Equisetum* 'Bandit' has alternating green and yellow bands along the shoots. These are sturdy and coarse, so with the different colours on them they form a good texture for a jungle garden. They can spread a bit, so it is best to grow them in a pot or contained border. *Equisetum* doesn't like drying out, so make sure it is watered regularly.

Eriobotrya japonica 'Okân'

Loquat

Origin:	Minimum temperature:
China	-15°C (5°F)
Position:	Maximum height:
Full sun to dappled shade	3m (10ft)

The loquat is mainly known for its sweet fruit, but it is also a great jungle plant for a sunny and dry garden. The large, lance-shaped leaves on the species are dark green, but the cultivar 'Okân' (which translates as yellow sun) has a golden variegation. It is an old Japanese selection, but only recently introduced into Europe.

F

Eucomis
Pineapple lily

Origin:	Minimum
South Africa	temperature:
	-10°C (14°F)
Position:	Maximum height:
Full sun to	15-120cm (6in–4ft)
dappled shade	

The pineapple lily has become more and more popular in recent years, ensuring that the release of new species and cultivars is surging. Although some, such as *Eucomis bicolor,* have flowers which smell of rotting flesh, others, such as 'Pink Gin', have sweet-smelling blooms. The leaves are linear and apart from green they can be speckled (*E. vandermerwei*) or dark red (*E. comosa* 'Sparkling Burgundy'). One giant amongst *Eucomis* is the species *pole-evansii* with the cultivar 'Goliath' in particular. This one can easily grow over 1.2m (4ft) tall and has huge flower spikes.

OPPOSITE—A dense clump of *Eucomis comosa* in the foreground backed by the dark red leaf of *Ensete ventricosum* 'Maurelii'.

Eupatorium capillifolium
Small dog fennel

Origin:	Minimum
North America	temperature:
	-5°C (23°F)
Position:	Maximum height:
Full sun to	2m (6½ft)
partial shade	

The *Eupatorium* species found in garden centres tends to be a tall perennial with big, pink flowers. *E. capillifolium,* however, is grown more for its very fine foliage. It doesn't like drying out, so if it is in a sunny position make sure it is well mulched and watered during dry spells. While it is not overly hardy, it can easily be overwintered by putting a few cuttings in a glass of water.

Farfugium japonicum 'Aureomaculatum'
Leopard plant

Origin:	Minimum
Japan	temperature:
	-10°C (14°F)
Position:	Maximum height:
Dappled shade	40cm (16in)
to full shade	

When I visited Tresco Abbey Garden on the Isles of Scilly, one of my earliest inspirations for jungle gardening, I came across this spotted *Farfugium.* It was growing under trees and appeared very exotic to me. There are now a few cultivars of this hardy perennial available but 'Aureomaculatum' is the most colourful one. The yellow spots stand out and will brighten up the shady corners in which they prefer to grow. They don't tolerate full sun or drying out, so a moisture-retentive spot in the shade is perfect. When grown in a pot it is best to place a saucer under the pot so the plant has a constant supply of water. If it does dry out the leaves will flop down but watering it will soon rejuvenate the plant.

Farfugium
japonicum 'Ryuto'

Leopard plant

Origin: *Japan*	Minimum temperature: *-10°C (14°F)*
Position: *Dappled shade to full shade*	Maximum height: *40cm (16in)*

The growth on the leaves of 'Ryuto' deserves a special mention. The surface of the leaves has lines which come together in a wart-like bundle of growth. The texture of this old Japanese cultivar is very alien and while some people love it, others are disgusted by it, which means it will always be a talking point in the garden. Like *Farfugium japonicum* 'Aureomaculatum', this cultivar is fully hardy and prefers a shady spot in moisture-retentive soil. It was recently introduced into Europe by modern day British plant hunter Kevin Hobbs.

Fatsia japonica
'Tsumugi-shibori'

Fatsia

Origin: *Japan*	Minimum temperature: *-15°C (5°F)*
Position: *Dappled shade*	Maximum height: *2m (6½ft)*

This *Fatsia* is often sold as 'Spider's Web' but 'Tsumugi-shibori' is the correct name, given by its breeder, Shigeru Kawarada. The glossy leaves have an intricate detail of white variegation on it, giving the plant a very bright appearance. In a garden with low light levels it will stand out and be a real eye-catcher. *Fatsia japonica* are very tough plants which will soon get to a decent size. They respond very well to hard pruning so if they become too large they can safely be cut back and will soon grow again. The flowers which appear late in the year are small but very attractive to bees.

Ficus carica

Fig

Origin: *Western Asia*	Minimum temperature: *-15°C (5°F)*
Position: *Full sun*	Maximum height: *4m (13ft)*

The common fig is very hardy and likes well-drained, poor soil. If it is grown for the jungle look it can be planted out and pruned to keep it in check. The palmate foliage on fig trees is very attractive, the cultivar 'Ice Crystal' (above) being especially stunning, with leaves that resemble a snowflake or ice crystal. It was a holiday find in Eastern Turkey by Cor van Gelderen of Esveld Nurseries. A very unusual and rare cultivar is *Ficus carica* 'Jolly Tiger'. The white variegation on this form gives the leaves a marbled effect. The white can scorch a little in full sunshine, so a position in slightly more dappled shade would be preferable for this one.

G   H

Ficus johannis
subsp. digitata

Fig

Origin:	Minimum
Iran/Afghanistan	temperature:
	-10°C (14°F)
Position:	Maximum height:
Full sun	*2m (6½ft)*

Ficus johannis subsp. *digitata* has beautiful foliage, with the green parts around the veins of the leaf so thin they are barely present. The palmate form and these thin leaf parts show why this variety was named *digitata*. Unlike *Ficus carica,* which is the more common fig, this plant does not grow very tall and is therefore suitable for growing in a pot. It likes a sunny aspect and doesn't want to stand too wet. Another silver-leaved member of this species, *F. johannis* subsp. *afghanistanica*, combines very well with dark succulents such as *Aeonium* 'Zwartkop'. The plants will produce figs but they will be smaller than the fruit produced by the more commonly known species *Ficus carica.*

Geranium
maderense

Giant herb-robert

Origin:	Minimum
Madeira	temperature:
	-5°C (23°F)
Position:	Maximum height:
Full sun to	*1m (3¼ft)*
dappled shade	

This tender geranium will form large, palmate leaves on red stems. It can grow quite large in a sunny, well-drained spot, so give it some space; it isn't very hardy, but on a south-facing wall it should survive most winters. Once it has produced its massive pink flowerheads it will die down completely. It can easily be grown from seed or will often self-seed after flowering.

Hakonechloa
macra 'All Gold'

Japanese forest grass

Origin:	Minimum
Japan	temperature:
	-20°C (-4°F)
Position:	Maximum height:
Dappled shade	*40cm (16in)*
to full shade	

Japanese forest grass is one of the finest grasses for a jungle garden, its linear leaves bending down gracefully and moving in the slightest breeze. This effect has given it the Japanese common name of 'Grass that knows the wind is blowing'. It loves dry shade and will not tolerate full sun as it will scorch the leaves. Cultivars such as 'Albostriata' which have more green in the leaf will take more sunshine exposure. The leaves turn a golden brown in winter and can be cut back in early spring to reveal the new shoots emerging.

Hedychium 'Dr Moy'

Variegated ginger lily

Origin: Nepal	**Minimum temperature:** -15°C (5°F)
Position: Dappled shade	**Maximum height:** 1.5m (5ft)

Hedychium are part of the ginger family and have lance-shaped leaves which, in the cultivar 'Dr Moy' (opposite), are subtly covered in white speckles. Some heavier variegated sports, such as 'Verity', have been selected from this cultivar. They are all hardy, but cutting the stems off before winter and placing these on the crown can give a bit of extra protection. *Hedychium* normally grow during the monsoon season, so if they don't get enough water with liquid fertilizer the plants may end up dying back to the ground to start a period of dormancy.

Helianthus salicifolius

Willow-leaved hardy sunflower

Origin: North America	**Minimum temperature:** -35°C (-31°F)
Position: Full sun to dappled shade	**Maximum height:** 2m (6½ft)

This perennial sunflower doesn't look anything like the familiar giant flower for most of the year; it's not until early to mid-autumn that the tiny sunflowers emerge from the tall stems. However, the thin, narrow foliage of this plant is beautiful from early spring to the first frost. When planted among shrubs it weaves its way through and finds support from them, but planted on its own it can flop over during summer, so support is needed. In winter the stems can be cut down to the ground. New shoots will emerge in spring.

Hosta

Hosta

Origin: China and Japan	**Minimum temperature:** -25°C (-13°F)
Position: Full shade	**Maximum height:** 10-100cm (4in–3¼ft)

The range of *Hosta* plants is extensive, but the care they need is generally the same; they don't like drying out and will grow best in a shady area on moisture-retentive soil. They are also very suitable to be grown in pots – miniature hostas such as *H. kikutii* var. *yakusimensis* or *H.* 'Blue Mouse Ears' in particular can make a lovely display. Large cultivars such as 'Sum and Substance' (above) or 'Empress Wu' will give a real impact with their massive leaves. Slugs are always a problem for hostas, but regular treatment of nematodes should keep this under control.

I

K

Iresine herbstii

Bloodleaf

Kalopanax septemlobus

Castor aralia

Impatiens omeiana 'Sango'

Busy lizzy

Origin:	Minimum
Japan	temperature:
	-15°C (5°F)
Position:	Maximum height:
Full shade	*30cm (12in)*

This hardy *Impatiens* does best on a moisture-retentive soil in shade; if it dries out it will die down completely until the soil is damp enough again. For this reason it is better grown in the garden than in a pot. In the right spot this plant will scramble through the garden and form a nice carpet of pink-variegated lance-shaped leaves.

Origin:	Minimum
South America	temperature:
	0°C (32°F)
Position:	Maximum height:
Full sun to	*60cm (2ft)*
dappled shade	

Iresine herbstii is a plant with attractive foliage that can be used in the dry and sunny jungle garden. It is easy to overwinter as cuttings in a glass of water and when potted up in spring they soon grow into nice-sized plants which will form a colourful display until late in the season. The cultivar with dark red and pink leaves is called 'Acuminata' (above) while 'Aureoreticulata' has green and yellow leaves.

Origin:	Minimum
South America	temperature:
	-20°C (-4°F)
Position:	Maximum height:
Full sun	*2m (6½ft) if*
	coppiced annually

Kalopanax septemlobus looks exotic but is a very hardy tree. The palmate leaves, up to 30cm (12in) long, have a strong shape and the stems have large spikes on them, giving extra architectural texture to the plant. In autumn the leaves turn a golden colour. This tree can grow to 10m (33ft) tall, but responds very well to coppicing. It can be grown in a pot as well as in open ground.

L

Kniphofia caulescens

Red-hot poker

Origin:	Minimum temperature:
South Africa	-20°C (-4°F)
Position:	Maximum height:
Full sun	60cm (2ft)

Kniphofia really stand out from the crowd with their linear foliage which, in the case of *K. caulescens*, is silver-blue; the cultivar 'Oxford Blue' (above) has the best colour of all. *K. caulescens* forms small stems which gradually elevate the plants above surrounding vegetation. They don't mind drying out and in the right position on well-drained soil they will produce arrow-like flowerheads which go from yellow at the bottom to orange-red at the top. Another great *Kniphofia* to grow for foliage is *K. northiae*. This can be a good alternative to *Agave* in colder climates.

Liriodendron chinense

Tulip tree

Origin:	Minimum temperature:
China	-20°C (4°F)
Position:	Maximum height:
Full sun to partial shade	3m (10ft) if coppiced annually

The common name for *Liriodendron* is tulip tree because of the shape of its flowers which are very exotic-looking in shades of orange, yellow and green. I first encountered *L. chinense* in the RHS gardens at Wisley where it is coppiced every year in order to produce larger leaves of a dark purple colour. Later in the year this colouration fades to green, but the size and shape of the leaves alone make this a perfect foliage plant. In autumn the leaves will turn a beautiful butter gold colour. When the tree is coppiced it won't produce flowers, but it can be grown in smaller gardens and will even tolerate being grown in a pot. It is very hardy but does not like drying out, so give it plenty of water and the occasional liquid seaweed feed when grown in a large pot. The species *L. tulipifera* has several white- and yellow-variegated cultivars.

Liriope muscari 'Okina'

Lily-turf

Origin:	Minimum temperature:
Japan	-20°C (-4°F)
Position:	Maximum height:
Dappled shade to full sun	25cm (10in)

Liriope is one of the best evergreen plants with linear foliage and comes in many colours, from green to nearly white. The cultivar 'Okina' is in a league of its own as the new foliage comes up pure white in spring. It retains that colour until midsummer, when it gradually turns to green. If the plant is grown in shade the white will last even longer. It doesn't require a lot of maintenance, but if there are dead leaves they can be pulled out in spring.

M

Melianthus major

Giant honey bush

Origin:	Minimum
South Africa	temperature:
	-10°C (14°F)
Position:	Maximum height:
Full sun	1.8m (6ft)

Melianthus major is a woody perennial which will die down in severe winters, but in mild ones it will retain its grey-blue foliage, which gives off a strong scent of peanuts. For winter protection in colder areas the shoots can be cut off after the first frost and placed over the base of the plant. It likes sunshine and does well on drier soils. Red flowers appear in early summer and are followed by very large seedpods. The cultivar 'Purple Haze' (above) has purple new growth and remains much smaller than the plain species. 'Purple Haze' should not be mollycoddled as overwatering and overfeeding will result in the plant gradually withering away. It was discovered in a batch of seedlings by Sean Hogan at the Dry Garden Nursery in California. *Melianthus villosum* is another species in the genus and is reported to be hardier than *M. major*. The leaves are light green and have a hairy surface.

Manihot grahamii

Tapioca tree

Origin:	Minimum
South America	temperature:
	-15°C (5°F)
Position:	Maximum height:
Full sun to	2m (6½ft)
light shade	

Manihot has a very unusual palmate shaped leaf which, when the plant gets more mature, forms a densely layered canopy. It looks quite delicate and can be grown in pots, but does best in the ground, where it will soon bulk up and the stems will become thicker, making them ideal cutting material for propagation. *Manihot* likes to be well fed on a free-draining soil, so a top-dressing of manure at the start of the growing season will make sure it soon grows to its full height. Together with *Brassaiopsis mitis*, *Manihot grahamii* takes top billing for 'most unusual leaf form'. It is a great plant which can be hard to get hold of, but it is certainly worth the extra effort of tracking it down. *Manihot* can be grown from seed very easily and has a good germination rate.

Mahonia eurybracteata subsp. ganpinensis 'Soft Caress'

Mahonia

Origin:	Minimum
Japan	temperature:
	-20°C (-4°F)
Position:	Maximum height:
Full sun to	1.2m (4ft)
dappled shade	

Normally *Mahonia* are very prickly plants, but this one is completely spine-free. It forms a small, evergreen shrub with yellow, scented flowers in late autumn/early winter. The long evergreen, feathered leaves form a strong texture in winter when other plants may have died down. 'Soft Caress' (opposite) also does very well in pots as it is naturally slow-growing. This *Mahonia* is very tolerant of a drier spot in the garden.

Musa basjoo

Japanese fibre banana

Origin: *Japan*	**Minimum temperature:** *-10°C (14°F)*
Position: *Dappled shade to full sun*	**Maximum height:** *4m (13ft)*

Musa basjoo is a herbaceous perennial, but its habit is more that of a multi-stemmed tree. The thick trunks can grow to 3m (10ft) tall and the paddle-shaped leaves can reach another metre (3ft). A good mulch, plenty of water and a regular liquid feed will enhance the growth rate of this plant. In warm and long summers a flower can appear from the centre of the crown (opposite). The base of this flower can be eaten the way artichokes are and the leaf itself is often used in oriental cooking. The plant is quite hardy on underground parts, but to retain the tall stems above ground in colder areas they are best wrapped in straw, held together by layers of hessian or garden fleece. The height and overhanging habit of this plant make it an ideal upper-canopy plant. In areas with strong winds the leaves may shred so a sheltered position would be preferable there.

Nicotiana glauca

Tree tobacco

Origin: *South America*	**Minimum temperature:** *-5°C (23°F)*
Position: *Full sun to dappled shade*	**Maximum height:** *2.5m (8¼ft)*

Nicotiana glauca is related to the plant used to make tobacco. The leaves of this species are entirely different, though, as they are leathery and blue-grey. In well-drained soils in a sunny position it grows very tall, forming a thick stem which makes sure it doesn't fall over in high winds, and can survive some cold snaps in winter. It is a good plant for a different colour and texture at the back of a border.

Ophiopogon japonicus

Lily turf

Origin: *Japan*	**Minimum temperature:** *-15°C (5°F)*
Position: *Dappled shade*	**Maximum height:** *25cm (10in)*

I first saw *Ophiopogon japonicus* at the King Edward VII Park in Lisbon, where it was used as groundcover throughout the gardens. In a more minimalistic jungle garden it can be used in a similar way, providing a green carpet under larger shrubs or trees. Dwarf forms such as 'Gyoku-Ryu' are used for the same reason in pots and will imitate a mossy undergrowth. The cultivar 'Spring Gold' (above) comes up with yellow leaves that tend to keep a good colour throughout the year. They are hardy, very easy to split and will gradually find their way through the garden without becoming invasive.

Oreocnide
pedunculata

False nettle bush

Origin:	Minimum
Taiwan, China	temperature:
	-10°C (14°F)
Position:	Maximum height:
Dappled shade,	2.5–5m (8¼–16ft)
full sun, sheltered	

Oreocnide pedunculata is a recently introduced member of the nettle family, without the stings. It will form a large shrub or small tree with glossy, green, lance-shaped leaves, which are red-brown when first unfurled. It has withstood temperatures as low as -10°C (14°F) but may tolerate lower temperatures than that. Edinburgh Botanical Gardens has grown one successfully for quite a few years in one of their unheated temperate glasshouses. The leaves of *Oreocnide* combine well with grasses such as *Hakonechloa macra* or the filigree leaf of *Adiantum venustum*. The nettle family is quite large and some great foliage plants from this family are constantly being introduced from Asia.

Oplopanax horridus

Devil's club

Origin:	Minimum
North America	temperature:
	-30°C (-22°F)
Position:	Maximum height:
Dappled shade	2m (6½ft)
to full shade	

This deciduous shrub has palmate leaves which can grow up to 50cm (20in) across. The stems are covered in spines. It prefers a moisture-retentive, well-drained soil in dappled to full shade. It is a plant that will provide great impact for the coldest gardens.

Oreopanax
dactylifolius

Oreopanax

Origin:	Minimum
Mexico	temperature:
	-5°C (23°F)
Position:	Maximum height:
Dappled shade	3m (10ft)

Oreopanax is a genus in the Araliaceae family, most of which will create a Jurassic look in the jungle garden. The large, palmate leaves of *O. dactylifolius* unfurl with a beautiful bronze colour and will turn dark green later in the year. This plant will grow into a large shrub or small tree, but will take its time in reaching great heights. *Oreopanax* prefer moisture-retentive soil in shade, do not tolerate full sun and will need a very sheltered position to come through winter.

P

Pelargonium 'White Mesh'

Pelargonium

Origin:	Minimum
South Africa	temperature:
	0°C (32°F)
Position:	Maximum height:
Full sun to	25cm (10in)
dappled shade	

Pelargoniums are very useful at the front of a border or as edging plants along a path. Some of them, such as the silver-leaved *Pelargonium sidoides*, are relatively hardy on dry soils. *Pelargonium* 'White Mesh', an ivy-leaved cultivar, is not hardy, but worth overwintering by cuttings. The leaves have a white lace-like pattern all over which will be especially prominent when the plant is given a bit more shade, where it will brighten up the bed. In full sun the leaves will turn almost completely green.

Persicaria microcephala 'Red Dragon'

Knotweed

Origin:	Minimum
China	temperature:
	-25°C (-13°F)
Position:	Maximum height:
Partial shade,	80cm (2½ft)
full shade	

This perennial, *Persicaria microcephala* 'Red Dragon' , is a great asset to the hardy jungle garden, being easy to grow and quickly forming a nice clump of 50–80cm (1¾–2½ft) tall shoots with dark red and grey colouration on the leaves. It is also very easy to propagate by putting some shoots in a glass of water. Often it comes up early in the year and will form a nice backdrop to lighter plants or can be used to create darker corners in the border. Other cultivars available in the Dragon range are 'Chocolate Dragon', 'Silver Dragon' and 'Night Dragon'.

Plectranthus 'Brunsendorf'

Silver spurflower

Origin:	Minimum
South Africa	temperature:
	-5°C (23°F)
Position:	Maximum height:
Full sun to	40cm (16in)
dappled shade	

Plectranthus is a good addition to the sunnier jungle garden. The leaves come in all sorts of colours, including variegated forms. The cultivar 'Brunsendorf', which has silver leaves with serrated edges, was found as a chance seedling in his collection by Steve Edney, the British National Plant Collection holder of *Plectranthus*, and named after Andrea Brunsendorf, Director of Outdoor Landscapes at Longwood Gardens in Pennsylvania. One of the parents of this plant is 'Silver Shield' which, in mild winters, can survive being left outside. It is very easy to strike cuttings of *Plectranthus*, which can be overwintered on a windowsill, or grown as a houseplant.

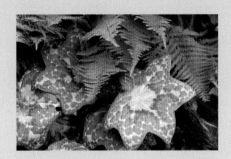

Podophyllum 'Kaleidoscope'

Mayapple

Origin: *Northern India/ China*	Minimum temperature: *-20°C (-4°F)*
Position: *Full shade*	Maximum height: *40cm (16in)*

Podophyllum is one of the best foliage plants for deep shade on a soil which doesn't dry out. The pattern of the foliage on cultivars such as 'Kaleidoscope' gives a very interesting texture to the border from early in the year. Slugs do enjoy the taste of these plants, so treatment with nematodes would be advisable. Apart from the cultivar 'Kaleidoscope' there is also 'Spotty Dotty', which is more readily available.

Pseudopanax ferox

Toothed lancewood

Origin: *New Zealand*	Minimum temperature: *-10°C (14°F)*
Position: *Full sun to dappled shade*	Maximum height: *3.5m (11½ft)*

Pseudopanax is a diverse genus with leaves resembling saw blades (*P. ferox* and *P. crassifolius*) or more palmate leaves (*P. lessonii* 'Gold Splash'). They are all evergreen and have thick, often glossy, leaves. *P. ferox* is quite unusual as it has two stages of leaf form. Plants up to about 2.5m (8¼ft) have linear, toothed leaves but once they grow taller the leaves become round and softer – the result of evolution as the tough lower leaves are a defence against foragers. Young shoots can be prone to aphid attacks as they have a sticky, protective layer on them which aphids like.

Puya chilensis

Chilean puya, sheep-eating plant

Origin: *Chile*	Minimum temperature: *-5°C (23°F)*
Position: *Full sun*	Maximum height: *50cm (20in)*

Puya chilensis (opposite, right) is a good plant for the sunny and dry jungle garden as it tolerates full sunshine and compact and dry soil. It forms a clump of very spiky, linear, grey leaves from which its name of sheep-eating plant is derived, as once sheep get stuck it is difficult for them to get away from the plant again. It is a very architectural plant that can produce huge flower spikes in very hot areas. However, it does take thirty years to flower, so until then, and in temperate climates, it should be considered as just a nice foliage addition of up to 50cm (20in) tall.

R

Reynoutria japonica 'Milk Boy'

Japanese knotweed

Origin: *Japan*	Minimum temperature: *-25°C (-13°F)*
Position: *Shade*	Maximum height: *80cm (2½ft)*

Japanese knotweed is a plant which puts fear into people's hearts as the green form is extremely invasive and when found in a garden can devalue the property. The white variegated form 'Milk Boy', however, is far less invasive and has attractive white-mottled, oval leaves with red stems. If a green shoot appears make sure to remove it and, although 'Milk Boy' is less invasive because of the white variegation, ensure it is only planted in a pot, preferably without a hole in the bottom so it can't escape into the garden soil. Cut out any flowers to prevent self-seeding and any plant material that needs to be disposed of should not be composted. If these precautions are taken you can enjoy a beautiful plant with leaves unlike anything else.

Rhus typhina Tiger Eyes ('Bailtiger')

Staghorn sumac

Origin: *North America*	Minimum temperature: *-20°C (-4°F)*
Position: *Full sun to dappled shade*	Maximum height: *2m (6½ft)*

Sumac trees can be invasive, but this cultivar is dwarf and does not sucker. The feathered yellow foliage looks as if it couldn't cope with sunshine, but I have successfully grown it in full sun where it thrived and there was no sign of scorch at all. Grown in shade, it will stay much smaller and will take a long time to get going. It is tolerant of drier soils. If the plant gets too big it can be cut down hard as it will soon shoot up again with bigger, more colourful leaves. It is a lovely plant to combine with darker leaves, especially as the autumn colours are bright red and yellow.

Robinia pseudoacacia 'Lace Lady'

False acacia

Origin: *North America*	Minimum temperature: *-30°C (-22°F)*
Position: *Full sun to dappled shade*	Maximum height: *0.5–2.5m (20in–8¼ft) (depending on graft point)*

This *Robinia* is the plant most asked about on the occasions when I open my garden to the public. All parts of it are twisted, from the branches to each individual leaflet on the feathered leaf. 'Lace Lady' is a dwarf form and the height of the main stem when you buy it determines the ultimate size. The smaller ones which are grown as shrubs are ideal for pots or at the top of a retaining wall, whereas the full standard sizes will grow into a small tree for the middle or rear section of a border. In spring the smallest twigs can be pruned out to make sure the main frame of the plant stays intact.

S

Rubus lineatus

Bramble

Origin: *China*	Minimum temperature: *-10°C (14°F)*
Position: *Dappled shade*	Maximum height: *2m (6½ft)*

While it is a bramble by name, *Rubus lineatus* is unlike any plant that grows in our hedgerows. *Rubus* is a very large genus with a lot of beautiful species that are suitable for a jungle garden. Apart from contributing unusual foliage, some of them, such as *Rubus phoenicolasius*, have stems covered in red hairs and spines, adding extra colour and texture to the border. The main feature of *R. lineatus* is the pleated palmate leaves. It does need a bit of space and grows best in a moisture-retentive soil that does not dry out at all, otherwise the leaves will drop off in summer. This plant can be thinned out or cut back entirely every year.

Sambucus nigra

Elderflower

Origin: *Europe*	Minimum temperature: *-25°C (-13°F)*
Position: *Full sun to full shade*	Maximum height: *3m (10ft)*

Elderflowers add attractive colour and texture to a border, with feathered leaves that may be green, yellow, purple or variegated. The cultivar 'Linearis' (above) has thread-like leaves and is slower-growing than most elderflowers. When coppiced every year it can shoot up to 2m (6½ft) and the long, winding shoots will weave their way through other large-leaved plants. For a darker, lace-like leaf the cultivar 'Eva' (Black Lace) is very graceful but will grow taller. Coppicing every year will produce larger, darker leaves.

Schefflera macrophylla

Umbrella tree

Origin: *Vietnam*	Minimum temperature: *-10°C (14°F)*
Position: *Full sun*	Maximum height: *3m (10ft)*

Although *Schefflera* have been grown as houseplants for many years, there have been some more recent introductions of hardy garden plants. *S. macrophylla* is one of the most dramatic ones. The large, palmate leaves have lance-shaped individual leaflets. It requires a sheltered, sunny position and can then easily reach 3m (10ft) in height.

Setaria palmifolia

Palm grass

Origin: *Asia*	Minimum temperature: *-5°C (23°F)*
Position: *Full sun to dappled shade*	Maximum height: *2m (6½ft)*

Although *Setaria palmifolia* is part of the grass family, the leaves, as its name suggests, resemble those of palm trees. The pleats on the leaves give them a very distinctive texture that forms a good combination with plants that have smooth, glossy leaves. The leaf edge is very sharp, so don't put *Setaria* along a path or patio. These plants don't like drying out but are happy beneath other plants, where they will scramble through the canopy to find the light. They can survive mild winters, or be placed in an unheated greenhouse, but for a higher survival chance they are better dug up and moved to a frost-free location for the cold season. They are easy to grow from seed or can be split when the clump gets too big.

Sinopanax formosanus

Sinopanax

Origin: *Taiwan, China*	Minimum temperature: *-15°C (5°F)*
Position: *Dappled shade*	Maximum height: *2m (6½ft)*

Although this *Sinopanax* is hardy to -15°C (5°F), for the first two or three years it's advisable to grow it in a pot and protect it during cold winters. In its natural habitat it can grow into a small tree, but in cooler areas it will take a very long time to reach that, so the 'ultimate' height is slightly lower. The fan-shaped leaves are thick and dark green, with serration along the edge.

Solanum pyracanthum

Porcupine tomato

Origin: *Madagascar*	Minimum temperature: *-1°C (30°F)*
Position: *Full sun to dappled shade*	Maximum height: *1m (3¼ft)*

Part of the very large nightshade family, which includes potatoes and tomatoes, *Solanum pyracanthum* is one of its spikiest members. The silver-grey foliage has bright orange spines on it, forming a striking contrast. It can survive outside in pots in very mild areas, where it may die down to the ground and shoot up from the base. However, it is very easy to grow from seed and the younger plants have larger leaves, which make it stand out more from the crowd. Another, even spikier *Solanum* is *S. atropurpureum*, which can grow up to 2m (6½ft) in one season and has stems and leaves covered in black spikes, giving it the common name of purple devil. This species can tolerate a bit more frost but is also very easy to grow from seed.

T

Sparrmannia africana

African hemp

Origin: *Southern Africa*	Minimum temperature: 5°C (41°F)
Position: *Dappled shade to full sun*	Maximum height: 2.5m (8¼ft)

The green form of *Sparrmannia africana* is a wonderful plant to have in a bright spot. Quite fast-growing, it has large, heart-shaped leaves which are covered in soft hairs, making it a beautiful backdrop for other planting. It likes a moisture-retentive soil which doesn't dry out completely. It can be overwintered as a houseplant. If it takes up too much space indoors then it can easily be cut down to 20cm (8in). New shoots will have appeared by the time it is ready to go out in the garden again. 'Variegata' (above) is a beautiful variegated form, but it does require a bit more looking after as it is prone to scorching and reverting so requires protection from the sun and keeping an eye out for new growth that reverts to the green form.

Strobilanthes dyeriana

Persian shield plant

Origin: *South-East Asia*	Minimum temperature: 5°C (41°F)
Position: *Dappled shade*	Maximum height: 40cm (16in)

The leaf colour of *Strobilanthes dyeriana* is highly unusual, with purple tones having a fluorescence over them which forms a contrast with everything else around. They are difficult plants to grow and therefore remain rare, although in the 1970s they were often used as houseplants. The best way to overwinter them is by taking cuttings and placing those in a jar of water out of direct sunlight until they root. I have never been able to grow them for more than two seasons, but if you can find one it is worth all the effort. Another *Strobilanthes* to look out for is *S. lactaea*, with dark green leaves and white markings. It is much easier to grow than *S. dyeriana* and also adds colour and texture to the border.

Tagetes lemonii

Marigold

Origin: *North America*	Minimum temperature: -5°C (23°F)
Position: *Full sun*	Maximum height: 1.2m (4ft)

This marigold is a shrubby relative of the plant which is often used as annual bedding. The leaves are extremely fragrant and the scent will be released when you brush past it, so planting it near a path is ideal. The feathered leaves are delicate and form a good combination with larger leaves. During mild winters it will flower from January onwards and won't die back at all. In colder areas it may die down, but will soon shoot up again in early spring; in these areas it is best to cut it down once the chance of frost has passed as the old shoots will provide some protection to the crown over winter. It is easily overwintered as cuttings by placing some in a glass of water where they will soon form roots.

Tetrapanax papyrifer 'Rex'

Rice-paper plant

Origin: *Taiwan, China*	**Minimum temperature:** *-10°C (14°F)*
Position: *Dappled shade to full sun*	**Maximum height:** *3–5m (10–16ft)*

Every jungle garden, large or small, should have a *Tetrapanax papyrifer* 'Rex'. The structure of the palmate leaves instantly gives the jungle look and once the plant is bigger it enhances the feeling of being immersed in a jungle too. It is quite fast growing but can sometimes be knocked back a bit by severe frosts – if cold weather is forecast it is wise to put some garden fleece over the crown. It will be deciduous in colder areas but the leaves will start appearing very early in spring. *T. p.* 'Rex' can branch out after a few years and will give protection from the sun for any plants growing under the large canopy. This is very dense because of the size of the leaves, which can get to 80–100cm (2½–3ft) across, so only shade-loving plants can grow beneath it.

Tolmiea menziesii 'Taff's Gold'

Piggyback plant

Origin: *North America*	**Minimum temperature:** *-20°C (-4°F)*
Position: *Full shade*	**Maximum height:** *20cm (8in)*

Tolmiea menziesii 'Taff's Gold' is often sold as a houseplant and it was one of the first plants I ever propagated, while I was in primary school. It is very easy to propagate by taking off a leaf, placing it on top of some compost and covering it with more compost, making sure the little leaflet in the middle still sticks above ground. The plant is very hardy and tolerant of the deepest shade, where it will form a dense carpet of yellow-mottled leaves, brightening up the darkest corners. The brown flowers are very attractive to bees.

Trachycarpus fortunei

Hardy palm tree

Origin: *China, Japan*	**Minimum temperature:** *-25°C (-13°F)*
Position: *Full sun to partial shade*	**Maximum height:** *5m (16ft) or more*

Trachycarpus fortunei is one of the hardiest palm trees and usually readily available. The beautiful palmate leaves are evergreen and quite sturdy so can withstand some wind too. It can be bought as a small plant for lower-level impact, but after a few years it will form a trunk and will gradually grow taller. Plants bought at a taller stage can sometimes take a few years to settle in and may look a bit scruffy at first. Any dying leaves at the bottom of the plant can be cut off in spring.

Tradescantia zebrina

Inch plant

Origin:	Minimum
Mexico, Guatemala	temperature:
	0°C (32°F)
Position:	Maximum height:
Dappled shade	20cm (8in)

The contrast of the purple and silver-striped lance-shaped leaves of this *Tradescantia* are a good eye-catcher at the front of a border, or on top of a retaining wall. The plant is very easy to propagate and if I have a gap in my border I just snap a few bits off the main plant and push them in the ground – within a week roots will appear and the plants will grow. It is not hardy but very easy to overwinter by just putting a few sprigs in a pot filled with compost or in a glass of water. A combination with black-flowering *Petunia* is always very striking.

Trevesia palmata

Snowflake tree

Origin:	Minimum
East Asia	temperature:
	-10°C (14°F)
Position:	Maximum height:
Dappled shade	3m (10ft)

The snowflake tree gets its name from the shape of the leaf and the fact that the new growth is covered in white dust, appearing like an ice crystal. The woody stems are spiky and the glossy, palmate leaves are very unusual, making it one of those shrubs that are on every jungle gardener's wish list. It can be successfully grown in pots, but make sure they don't stand in water during winter as the roots will rot.

Tricyrtis hirta 'Variegata'

Toad lily

Origin:	Minimum
Japan	temperature:
	-25°C (-13°F)
Position:	Maximum height:
Full shade	70cm (2¼ft)

Toad lilies are very hardy and yet exotic-looking perennials. The lance-shaped leaves on the species *Tricyrtis hirta* are hairy, whereas *T. formosana* has glossy leaves. They quickly bulk up in the darkest corners of the garden. The variegated cultivar *T. hirta* 'Variegata' has a neat silver line around the leaf edge which highlights the shape of the leaves. The flowers are like a small lily flower with dark pink spots all over them.

V Z

Verbesina alternifolia

Wingstem

Origin: North America	Minimum temperature: -20°C (-4°F)
Position: Full sun to dappled shade	Maximum height: 2.5m (8½ft)

The large leaves of this very hardy perennial are a great backdrop to any jungle border. The leaf resembles a *Quercus rubra* (red oak) leaf, but is coarse and has silver veins, giving extra visual interest and texture. The common name reflects the leaf-like lines which go all the way up the stems. *Verbesina alternifolia* likes sun to dappled shade in moist soil. The soil needs to be rich in nutrients. On poorer soil manure needs to be added for it to produce its height and lush foliage.

Zingiber mioga 'White Feather'

Ginger

Origin: China/North Vietnam	Minimum temperature: -15°C (5°F)
Position: Dappled shade	Maximum height: 80cm (2½ft)

Out of the variegated gingers, 'White Feather' (opposite) is one of the better-growing cultivars, with good hardiness. The leaves are lance-shaped and their thin, white margins light up darker corners in the garden. Because the variegation along the edge of the leaf covers a small area, the plant is still a strong grower. In colder winters it can take a bit longer to come up again; a late autumn mulch will protect it from the harshest frosts and will ensure moisture retentiveness for the drier summer months.

Typhonium horsfieldii

Artist's aroid

Origin: Asia	Minimum temperature: -10°C (14°F)
Position: Full shade	Maximum height: 25cm (10in)

Typhonium horsfieldii has lance-shaped leaflets which form the entire leaf in an unusual semi-circle. It loves deep shade and grows well in a pot as long as it doesn't dry out too much. If planted out in the ground it will soon form a nice clump. It can self-seed, so place it in an area where it can roam around to find its ideal position.

Resources

United Kingdom

BIOLOGICAL CONTROL

Dragonfli
dragonfli.co.uk

NURSERIES

Architectural Plants
Stane Street
North Heath
Pulborough, West Sussex
RH20 1DJ
architecturalplants.com

Cotswold Garden Flowers
Sands Lane
Badsey
Evesham
WR11 7EZ
cgf.net

Crûg Farm Plants
Griffith's Crossing
Caernarfon
Gwynedd
LL55 1TU
Wales
crug-farm.co.uk

Desert to Jungle
Henlade Garden Nursery
Lower Henlade
Taunton
TA3 5NB
deserttojungle.com

Hardy Exotics
Gilly Lane
Whitecross
Penzance
TR20 8BZ
hardyexotics.com

Jurassicplants Nurseries
Waen Road
Saint Asaph
Denbighshire
Wales
LL17 0DY
jurassicplants.co.uk

Newbury Farm Plants
Ampthill Road
Silsoe
Bedfordshire
MK45 4HB
newburyfarmplants.co.uk

Palm Centre
Ham Central Nurseries
Ham Street
Ham, Richmond
TW10 7HA
www.palmcentre.co.uk

Pan-Global Plants
The Walled Garden
Frampton Court
Frampton-on-Severn
GL2 7EX
panglobalplants.com

Penberth Plants
penberthplants.co.uk

Pineview Plants
Pineview
19 Windmill Hill
Wrotham Heath
Kent
TN15 7SU
pineviewplants.co.uk

Plant Base
Sleepers Stile Road
Wadhurst
East Sussex
TN5 6QX
plantbase.co.uk

Swines Meadow Farm Nursery
47 Towngate E
Market Deeping
Peterborough
PE6 8LQ
swinesmeadowfarmnursery.co.uk

Trebah Plant Centre
Mawnan Smith
Falmouth, Cornwall
TR11 5JZ
trebahgarden.co.uk

Trecanna Nursery
Chilsworthy
Gunnislake
PL18 9PB
trecanna.com

Urban Jungle
Ringland Lane
Old Costessey
Norwich
NR8 5BG
urbanjungle.uk.com

Belgium

BIOLOGICAL CONTROL

Ecostyle
ecostyle.be

NURSERIES

Andrew's Garden
Kantestraat 3B
8700 Kanegem
andrewsgarden.be

Canna-banana
Tinstraat 72B
2580 Putte
canna-banana.be

France

NURSERIES

Pépinière AOBA
La Touche au Burgot
35460 Saint Quen la Rouerie
pepiniere-aoba.com

Pépinière de la Roche St Louis
Roche Saint Louis
7 Les Trois Moineaux
44680 Saint Pazanne
pepiniere-roche-saint-louis.fr

Germany

NURSERIES

Der Palmenmann
(webshop only)
palmenmann.de

Fesaja (webshop only)
fesaja-versand.de

Flora Toskana
Schillerstr. 25
89278 Nersingen
flora-toskana.com

Palme per Paket
Tobias W. Spanner
Am Schnepfenweg 57
80995 München
palmeperpaket.de

Raritätengärtnerei
Jan Kalivoda
Eckerstrasse 32a
933471 Arnbruck

The Netherlands

BIOLOGICAL CONTROL

Ecostyle
ecostyle.nl

NURSERIES

Bandus
Sliekstraat 9
6999 DX Hummelo
bandus.nl

Coen Jansen
Ankummeres 13A
7722 RD Dalfsen
coenjansenvasteplanten.nl

Exoterra
Meulereed 2
8421 PP Oldeberkoop
exoterra.nl

Kwekerij aan de Dijk
Dijkweg 99
9984 NX Oudeschip
kwekerijaandedijk.nl

Plantenkwekerij de Zwart
Haling 5
1619 PT Andijk
plantenkwekerijdezwart.nl

Tuingoed Foltz
Hereweg 346
9651 AT Meeden
tuingoedfoltz.nl

Thank you

Thank you to: publisher Anna Mumford of Filbert Press, photographer Sarah Cuttle and designer Michelle Noel for supporting the idea and creating this beautiful book; Francine Raymond, who helped me with my book proposal; Roy Lancaster for pointing me in Anna's direction and being a life-long inspiration; my mother Tanja Oostenbrink-de Groot for finding information for the plant profiles (working out those temperature zones is a pain!); Kevin Hobbs for helping me find interesting new plants to talk about; Mercy Morris for tagging along to nurseries to buy more plants and confirming plant names for me; Tom Hart Dyke for writing the foreword and the endless jungle plant chats over the years; and Pete Richardson for taking me to Will Giles's garden and changing my life in the jungle forever.

Thank you to my grandmother, my father and my uncle Hendrik for passing on their love of plants and gardening to me.

Thanks also to the following garden owners and designers for opening their garden to us:

Jungle Living
Antonia Schofield, garden designed by Antonia Schofield Garden Design, antoniaschofield.com

The Contemporary Jungle Garden
Jeroen Bergman, garden designed by Alex Mitchell, alex-mitchell.co.uk

The Garden Room
Phil King and Graham Clayton, garden designed by Antonia Schofield Garden Design, antoniaschofield.com

The Potted Jungle
Matthew Pottage

The Shady Jungle
Anna Anderson, garden designed by Wayne Simon Page, fabotanic.com

The Arid Jungle
Paul Spracklin

The Botanical Jungle
Mike Clifford

A City Oasis
Wayne Amiel

Finally, thank you to:

Joanne Bernstein, joannebernstein-gardendesign.com
Paul Carey and Phil Gomm
Louise Dowle and Steve Edney
Tim Hill
Janet Maxwell
Jo Naiman
Chris and Erika Savory
David and Elizabeth Smith
Jack Wallington

PICTURE CREDITS

Gerald Abrahams, page 15 (bottom right), page 154-57.
Daniel Hatch, page 17 (top).
Matt Payne, page 14, page 15 (top), page 17 (bottom right).
Philip Oostenbrink 12 (bottom), 84, 173, 174 (left), 176 (middle), 187 (middle), 190 (right), 191 (right), 193 (middle), 197 (middle), 198 (left & right), 199 (left & right), 204 (left), 210 (middle), 212 (middle).

Index

Page numbers in *italic* refer to pictures and those in **bold** refer to A–Z plant entries.

L

ladybirds 18
lanceolate (lance-shaped)
   leaves 31, 102
layering plants 59, 70–3, 150
light and dark foliage 70–1,
   100, 111
linear leaves 29, 107
Liriodendron 161
   chinense 161, **199**
   tulipifera 199
Liriope muscari 'Okina' 29, **199**
living walls 54, 60, 61
Lobelia
   bambuseti 76
   laxiflora var. *angustifolia* 45
Loropetalum chinense var.
   rubrum 'Fire Dance' 124, 125

M

Magnolia grandiflora 110, 111
Mahonia eurybracteata subsp.
   ganpinensis 'Soft Caress'
   30, 127, **201**
Manihot grahamii 29, 67, 150,
   201
Matteuccia struthiopteris 63,
   63
Melianthus
   major 33, 82, **201**
      'Purple Haze' 201, *201*
   villosum 201
Metasequoia glyptostroboides
   120
minimalist plantings 56–7,
   110–13
Miscanthus sinensis 26
momijigari 27
Muehlenbeckia complexa
   'Tricolor' 33
mulching 88
Musa 13, 25
   basjoo 14, 32, 57, 84, 85, 86,
      86, 114, 115, 115, 116, 167
Musella lasiocarpa 32, 166, 167

N

naturalism 50–3
nematodes 165
Neopanax laetus 82
Nicotiana glauca 33, **202**
nitrogen 160
Nymphaea pygmaea 96

O

Olea europaea 83, 129
Ophiopogon 27
   jaburan 'Vittatus' 123
   japonicus 12, 102, **202**
   japonicus 'Gyoku-Rhu' 202
   japonicus 'Nanus Variegatus'
      118, 119
   japonicus 'Spring Gold' 29,
      202, *202*
   planiscapus 'Nigrescens'
      124
Oplopanax horridus 102, **204**
Opuntia 189
Oreocnide pedunculata 31, **204**
Oreopanax dactylifolius 204
Osmanthus regalis 103
oval leaves 33
overwintering 166–7

P

paddle-shaped leaves 32, 84
palmate leaves 29, 59, 84, 107
paths 68, 70, 98, 135, 145, 146,
   152, 155
Paulownia 161
   tomentosa 107, *107*
Pelargonium 165
   sidoides 205
   'White Mesh' 38, *38*, **205**
pergolas 139
Persicaria
   microcephala 'Chocolate
      Dragon' 205
   microcephala 'Night Dragon'
      205
   microcephala 'Red Dragon'
      31, 62, *62*, 70, *103*, 164, **205**
   microcephala 'Silver Dragon'
      205
   runcinata 'Purple Fantasy'
      62, *62*
pesticides 165
pests and diseases 165
Petasites 162
   japonicus subsp. *giganteus*
      143

Petunia 213
Phoenix canariensis 128, 129
Phormium 13, 29, 57, *57*, 107,
   128, 129
   tenax 13
photosynthesis 100, 160
Phyllostachys 168
   aurea 115, 116, 117, *168*
   nigra 155, 168
pine 27
Pittosporum 13
plant size 117
planting density 54, 57, 68–9,
   73
Platycladus orientalis 'Franky
   Boy' 67, *150*
Plectranthus
   'Brunsendorf' 33, **205**
   'Silver Shield' 205
Podachaenium eminens 135
Podocarpus 123
Podophyllum 100
   'Kaleidoscope' **207**
   versipelle 'Spotty Dotty'
      48, 63, *63*, 102, 124, 125,
      127, 207
Polystichum 60, 61
   setiferum 102
ponds 96–7, 125
pot-grown plants 18, 88, 100,
   118–23, 149
   bamboo 168
   feeding 160
   pests 165
   potting up 163
   soil 160
   succulents 92
Prunus cerasifera 'Nigra' 146
Pseudopanax
   crassifolius 86, 207
   ferox 29, 53, 127, **207**
   lessonii 'Gold Splash' 207
Puya chilensis 29, **207**

R

repetition 117, 143
Reynoutria japonica 163
   'Milk Boy' 33, **208**
   var. *compacta* 'Variegata'
      120
Rhododendron 33
   'Elizabeth Lockhart' 33, 59,
      59
Rhus 33
   typhina Tiger Eyes
      ('Bailtiger') 33, 153, **208**
Robinia 96
   pseudoacacia 'Frisia' 143
   pseudoacacia 'Lace Lady'
      33, 64, *64*, **208**
round leaves 30
Rubus
   lineatus **209**
   phoenicolasius 209

S

Saccharum officinarum var.
   violaceum 164
St Michael's Mount, Cornwall
   89, *89*
Sambucus nigra **209**
   f. *porphyrophylla* Black
      Tower ('Eiffel 1') 33, 70, *150*,
      151
   'Linearis' 209, *209*
Sanicula epipactis 'Thor' 27
scale insects 165
scent 42, 45, 97
Schefflera 139, 167
   delavayi 139
   macrophylla 25, 75, *75*, 140,
      209
   taiwaniana 87
Sedum 92
   rupestre 'Angelina' 92
Selaginella kraussiana 127, *127*
Sempervivum arachnoideum
   12, *12*
Setaria palmifolia 29, **210**
shade
   creating 82, 96–9
   dappled 84, 96–9, 169
   komorebi 25, 84
   moisture retention 82, 96
   shady sites 100–3, 124–7
   upper canopy 80, 84–7, 96
Sinopanax formosanus 32, **210**
sites
   creating dappled shade 84,
      96–9, 168
   damp sites 88, 91, 100
   drainage 89, 91–3, 129, *133*
   dry 80–3, 84, 88–95, 128–33

T

U

V

W

Y

Z

ABOUT THE AUTHOR

Philip Oostenbrink was born in the Netherlands and began gardening at the age of four in his parents' allotment and grandmother's garden. The jungle plant obsession took hold after a trip to Tresco on the Isles of Scilly and a visit to the late Will Giles's spectacular exotic garden in Norwich. After teaching horticulture and running a gardening business, Philip moved to Kent first as Deputy Head Gardener at Hadlow College and then as Head Gardener at Canterbury Cathedral. He is now Head Gardener at Walmer Castle where one of his first projects has been to plant a jungle garden in the moat. Philip gives talks to gardening groups, leads garden tours, writes for gardening magazines and holds four National Plant Collections. At home in Kent he has created an idyllic urban jungle which featured on BBC TV Gardeners' World.